Washing Our Hands in the Clouds

To

9-3-18

Joe williams
Bo Petunz

Washing Our Hands

Joe Williams, His Forebears,
and Black Farms in South Carolina

in the Clouds

Bo Petersen

The University of South Carolina Press

Published by the University of South Carolina Press
Columbia, South Carolina 29208

www.sc.edu/uscpress

Manufactured in the United States of America

24 23 22 21 20 19 18 17 16 15   10 9 8 7 6 5 4 3 2 1

Library of Congress Cataloging-in-Publication Data can be
found at http://catalog.loc.gov/.

ISBN: 978-1-61117-551-6 (paperback)
ISBN: 978-1-61117-552-3 (ebook)

This book was printed on recycled paper with 30 percent
postconsumer waste content.

In memory of Celestine Williams.
Dedicated to our families.

Contents

Illustrations   *viii*

Preface   *ix*

Chapter 1—Right in the Heart   *1*

Chapter 2—Brick Bats   *13*

Chapter 3—Aunt Lou   *21*

Chapter 4—Blood Brothers   *31*

Chapter 5—Cockleburs   *37*

Chapter 6—Washed in the Clouds   *47*

Chapter 7—Tough Love   *61*

Chapter 8—The Money Crop   *71*

Chapter 9—The Last Plantation   *83*

Chapter 10—The Whole-Hog Year   *96*

Chapter 11—Legacy   *106*

Chapter 12—Home   *117*

Chapter 13—The House with Slaves   *124*

Chapter 14—An Aroma like Sweet Grass   *135*

Sources   *149*

Index   *151*

Illustrations

Joe Williams   *xii*

The Pee Dee of South Carolina   2

Bethea cotton press   7

Geraldine Williams   29

Jimmy Moody and Joe Williams   35

Irene and Copeland Moody   45

Letters Testamentary of Scipio Williams   57

Celestine and Joe Williams   73

Joe Williams   133

Preface

I'm not big on the word "serendipity." It's a little too happy-go-lucky a notion of chance, which is spontaneous, sure, but seems to come directed to you as much as out of nowhere. I like Albert Einstein's saying, "Coincidence is God's way of remaining anonymous."

I didn't know Randy Moody, but I met Joe Williams because Randy Moody thought he knew me. It happens in the business. I work for the newspaper he reads. He liked my writing and thought he recognized my name as a fellow church member. Well, I wasn't, but in the course of the conversation talk turned to Joe, the kid who had come to live on Randy's family farm. Joe's story riveted me: raised in a tenant shack, taken in as a young teen by a white family in the racial turmoil of the '60s, goes on to farm some of the biggest acreage a man could farm singlehandedly, while holding down a full-time job. I didn't know yet about Scipio Williams and Joe's singular heritage.

A few months later I sat in a bookstore coffee shop with Randy, Joe, and Jimmy Moody, the farmer who took Joe on as a worker, then as a brother, and now as a lifelong friend.

A few things struck me right away about Joe. He was quiet at first, letting Randy do a lot of the talking, but quick to jump in to correct something if Randy hadn't quite gotten it straight. Joe has a mind for numbers, recollecting years and sometimes specific dates uncannily, considering these were things that happened almost a half-century before. His memory is vivid, something that shows particularly when he talks about machines. He doesn't just remember a car or a tractor from forty-some years ago; he sees in his mind its color and interior and details about its engine.

When I got to talking with him, something else struck. He and I are about the same age, born within days of each other a year apart. So, despite the different circumstance of our upbringings, we share what the brains like to call a world view. We came along through the same times, with vantage points that weren't all that far removed. We know each other. We share a lot of core values, despite those different circumstances.

I originally titled this book simply *Joe*. What fascinates me about his story is that to all appearances he's an ordinary guy—and what a life.

Joe is the great-great-grandson of a freedman farmer who came into his own during the Civil War years when freedmen's very freedom, not to mention their land, was in jeopardy. Scipio Williams became a wealthy man in the midst of land and crop crises and is said to have met with Abraham Lincoln in the White House.

Joe's life turned out remarkably similar. He was pitted against a market that squeezed the little guys until they couldn't breathe and struggled against discriminatory federal lending practices that were supposed to help him, practices that led to the signature *Pigford v. Glickman* lawsuit.

His tale is the ways of the people who know him, of the storied Little and Great Pee Dee Rivers, where he lives, It's a story the ranges across bladderworts, grape Kool-Aid, and the Cape Fear Arch. It peels back a few layers of the obscure history of Lincoln's interactions with freed people.

It's staggering how profoundly his experiences echo larger, and largely undertold, social issues of when and where he came along.

These days are hi-def times. We blow up celebrities as heroes and exalt them like icons. In real life there are people you meet who wouldn't stand out in a crowd but astound you as you get to know them. They are your real icons, the markers in your life. Joe Williams is one.

Here's your chance to say, hey.

———

Washing Our Hands in the Clouds isn't your usual academic work and isn't meant to be. It's designed to read the way stories get told on a porch in conversation, the way I heard a lot of it: One thread opens up on another, eventually to wind up a complete quilt. I have a naturalist bent, and I wanted to put Joe Williams completely in his environment, telling his story in with tales of the Pee Dee itself and the history of the region that created the place where he lives. To see someone whole, I believe you have to see him or her in situ.

I didn't footnote because nobody footnotes a porch conversation. A lot of the information that would be footnoted in an academic book I wove into place using multiple sources, including my own background knowledge and experiences. The sources are listed in at the end of the book. When information came from a single source, I noted the source in the course of relating the information.

I am indebted to so many people for *Washing Our Hands in the Clouds* that a list would read like one of those interminable Oscar speeches. Among them are the late Celestine Williams; my wife, Cathy; and our respective families, who put up with this out-of-town collaboration for four years. Also, the Post and Courier and Evening Post Industries of Charleston, whose employment opened me to the lowcountry and the region's proud history, as well as to very cool stories such as the Georgetown canal. To the people of Latta and Temperance Hill, who graciously heard out a stranger and then helped out. They did it on little more than the trust that, if he was good by Joe Williams, he was good by them.

I probably couldn't come up with a complete list of people who scratched up the little glints of light to keep me fumbling along after the historical records of Scipio Williams. One of the first walls I had to get past was the problem of finding some sort of verification independent of the family's memory that Scipio Williams lived the remarkable life they talk about. I wasn't sure anything like that existed. Early on in the effort, Harlan Greene, of the Avery Research Center in Charleston, gave me a huge boost of confidence and pointed me to the Marion County archives. When the archivist brought out the thick envelope full of Letters Testamentary, I looked at Joe and said, "We just struck gold."

I'm grateful for guidance of Eldred Prince, whose *Long Green* was invaluable to me, to Erik Calonius of the College of Charleston and Doug Pardue of *The Post and Courier*, who weighed on massaging the manuscript. I can't express my gratitude to Alex Moore, Linda Fogle, and the staff at the University of South Carolina Press. For the Lincoln history, each historian I contacted trying to ferret out snatches of obscure Lincoln history was generous and genuinely interested in Scipio's story; they were all of no end of encouragement to me. I can't thank them—or anyone else who helped—enough. I'd be remiss not to give props to the historian and author Eric Foner. He had no particular reason to respond to a blind e-mail sent by a wannabe writer asking for one of the innumerable sources he had dug through for *The Fiery Trial*. But he did. His response led me to the names of the five North Carolina ministers documented to have called on the president. I had sought those names for three years; not knowing them left a huge loose end in the story: I could tell the reader that Somebody from Scipio's greater community had called on Lincoln, but I couldn't say if it was him. That one of the names turned out to be a Jarvis Williams leaves the sort of loose end that dangles tantalizingly.

Joe Williams and his tractor. Courtesy of Benton Henry Photography.

Chapter 1

Right in the Heart

Now faith is the substance of things hoped for, the evidence of things unseen.

Hebrews, 11:1

Joe, he ain't scared of the devil. I've never seen anybody with as much guts and determination as he has. If he had to call the devil up and make an appointment with him, he would do it.

Virginia Merchant, Joe William's friend

HIS HANDS ARE SOFT, no small thing in a man who has worked with his hands from the time he was four years old. His eyes get thoughtful before he speaks. They light up as he talks and his voice gets louder. He repeats himself and sometimes tends to stutter. He has since he was a child.

Joe Williams pulls his blue Toyota truck onto a dirt road in the old Boise Cascade timberlands along the Great Pee Dee River, what he calls the Pee Dee farm and the town still calls the old Cotton Grove plantation. This is where he made himself. He'd get home from a shift job at five or six o'clock at night, hop on the tractor, and work until ten or eleven o'clock. He'd get home on Friday and run the tractor work all night long, if he didn't have to work a Saturday day shift. All night long. He'd go home at seven o'clock in the morning—an hour or more after the sun came up. He'd sleep until one or two in the afternoon, jump back on the tractor, and run it until nearly midnight, when he finally gave out.

"So I know what work is," he says, nodding to it. "I know what work is. God knows I have done it. I spent a lot of days back up in here."

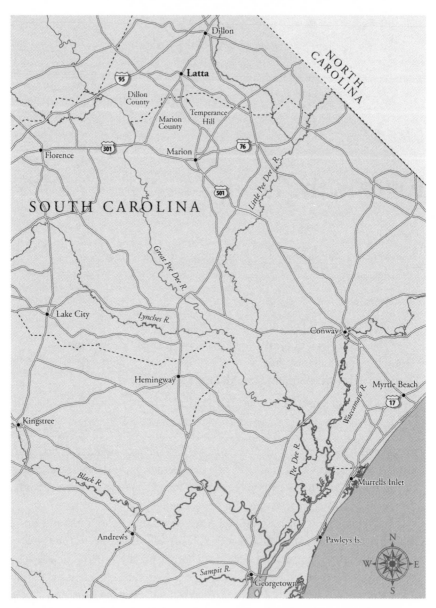

The Pee Dee of South Carolina is the northeast region surrounding the Great and Little Pee Dee Rivers. Latta, Joe Williams's hometown, is nestled in it. Courtesy of Gill Guerry.

THE STORY IS TOLD THROUGHOUT Joe's family: They are descended from a freedman farmer and craftsman who became a wealthy landowner in the Pee Dee. Joe's great-great-grandfather, Scipio Williams, distinguished himself enough that he met with Abraham Lincoln in the kitchen of the White House.

Joe was eleven years old when he first heard the story, one night late in the winter, by the heater in his grandfather's house, where he stayed as a child. Joe's mother lived there with six other children before she moved about a mile down the Ebenezer Road, to "just a plain country house, you know, no, no rest room in it, a house back by the woods, you know what I mean. No running water. That's how it was."

Scipio became Joe's measure of himself, the man he would live up to. Joe would go on to farm one of the largest spreads of land in the region among people of his background. He would buy back and plant on his great-great-granddad's land. And out of his life would come echo after echo of his forbearer's life, the barriers and biases he faced, the chances they took, the consequences. Side by side, their lives look like two rows of the same crop.

Here, pull up a chair. The Pee Dee is one of those country places where tales still get told on the porch. This one is a jaw dropper.

———

JOE'S FACE has the steady composure of a working man, his eyes a darting restlessness. He leans forward over the steering wheel of the bouncing truck and points with his arm to where his fields started. His eyes light up. He can see it again, the corn and the sweet corn, sweet potatoes, wheat, soybeans. And the fewer rows of tobacco. He was farming more than a thousand acres here at one point, while he held down that wage job. He ran a tractor by the lights night after night. He used to ride with a loaded pistol in the tractor glove compartment because he was way back off the paved road, back in the field off one of the dirt back roads that dropped to the river bottoms, back along the woods on land that was open to poaching.

"People come through here late at night. They've been drinking. Some kid'd shot you back here," His voice gets a little quicker as he says it. "Nobody'd never know what happened."

Joe's troubles came from behind, sometimes from the very people in farming who were supposed to have his back—something that would have left his great-great-grandfather weightily shaking his head.

Joe slows the truck by the scrub growth along a narrow, rainy weather run. His eyes roam the laid-out acres as he points.

"All right. I used to farm, starting here, everything both sides of the road, everything you see in here, far as you could see, both sides of the road. Picture it, just fields. Just fields, that's what this was, just old farm land," he says, his tongue drawing the last word out. "All that, that was open. All that over there was open. Both sides of the road, as far as you could see."

The land is grown in, runs of weeds and scraggles of skinny pine, a few volunteer crop plants sticking up.

———

THE PEE DEE ENVIRONS around Latta, South Carolina, where Joe Williams lives, tell a sort of a parable. At first the land seems ordinary, laid out for miles as if someone had plumbed it with a level. Then you notice the rumples, the simple folds where it falls to a swamp or creek. Then you get this hair-on-the-back-of-your-neck sensation that it's rising, a sense of plateau. An old stone and wood farmhouse under the leaning oak seems to be set in slope like a mountain home.

And you aren't mistaken. The region is the southern expanse of the Cape Fear Arch, one of those geological freaks you've never heard of. It's a tectonic lifting underground, coming up a centimeter or two per year along a diagonal line from the North Carolina mountains to Cape Fear along the North Carolina–South Carolina border.

It does something to the place.

The arch began climbing 35 to 45 millions of years ago during the Cretaceous Age, as intrinsic to the environs as the ocean floor sand and limestone that today define the sandhills along the states' border between the Piedmont and the coast. The lift literally pushes up the Pee Dee region as far south as Cape Romain, just north of Charleston. It is part of the reason why the lowcountry around Charleston is a seismic hot spot. The rub of the edge of the uplift against other underground features, the "hinge zone," creates what Robert Weems of the U.S. Geological Survey called a scissorslike compression on two faults that open on each other under the Ashley River—ground zero for the catastrophic 1886 earthquake.

The push might be infinitesimal, but it gives the place a presence. Rivers like the Pee Dee seem to run off it like foothills streams, depositing beds of relatively rich loam through the clay and sand country. Those beds lie in with the region's "bays," freshwater wetlands likely formed ages ago by a retreating ocean, to create a mix of what Joe calls heavy land and light land. "Heavy" is the richer growing soil. The mix is so pervasive that soil maps look mottled. The influences are subtle but striking. The Pee Dee region has a curious biological diversity—dozens of plant species are found in the Waccamaw basin just east of Latta that are not found anywhere else.

It's funny how right in the heart of something ordinary you find something so extraordinary. You find that in people, too.

———

FOLKS WHO HAVE KNOWN JOE all his life and know the Williams family go blank when asked if they have heard about Scipio Williams.

"Good gracious, that's back in the cowboy and Indian days," says lifelong friend George Legette.

Old Abe, a century and a half later, still isn't much of a hero for a lot of people in the South. Told the Lincoln story, J. G. Bryant, a farmer Joe has looked up to all his life, and Alex Johnson, his high school assistant principal, both get quiet. Later they seize on a remark that the War between the States was fought over the cotton economy, not slaves. They begin adamantly pushing a book they read that debunks the Lincoln "myth," written by a man they heard speak. Lincoln didn't want to free the slaves. No one will publish the man's book, they say. No one wants to disabuse the Lincoln myth.

In Joe's family the Lincoln story is legacy. Asked about Scipio Williams, Geraldine, Joe's mother, says simply, "He and Abe Lincoln was friends." She leans forward from the porch chair as she says it, and her gray eyes peer.

———

THE PEOPLE IN LATTA like to tell you it once was known as "the gentlemen farmer's town," huge spreads of fields and old family names that built plantation-style manors. And the trim to the crop fields running road to road feels like that. In the spring myriad dandelions sprout like sunshine. On a hot summer afternoon, grasshoppers and butterflies leap from the soybean, and when you move from the sun into wetland shade it feels like someone opened a cooler of ice.

It wasn't just a sales pitch when the form nominating the place for the National Register of Historic Places in 1984 said, "Latta has continued to be a small but stable community which retains much of its early twentieth century character." The town of Latta is a railroad town, one of those tiny places that seem stuck out in the middle of nowhere in today's interstate highway system of suburbs. On the first look around, most of the people I know would say there's nothing there. What is there is its people, and when they're your people you're home.

The town museum, naturally, has an old rail car. The rail is so embedded in the consciousness of the place that when the train horn wails, conversations lapse, pause, and fall into the rhythm of the passing train.

For a generation or so, Latta was a "stopping in" country town, one in the lines of such places along roads between the urban north and the white gold sands of Florida. Its modest motels and restaurants became the retail economy of the place. Then the interstates came, with surveyors looking for open land down through the rural South. I-95 was laid out just a few miles to the west of town, a few too many. So, like a lot of small towns in the region, Latta was left to the side, any real chance of economic development diverted, its farm character intact. Good or bad, that provided for the life Joe lives.

Today the surveyor ribbons are back, for I-73. This time the mother lode is the South Carolina beach, and the stakes are being driven right through the heart of the community.

The Pee Dee is a region of long-hoed tradition, like a lot of places in the agrarian South. Circa 1750, white Baptists founded a church down by Catfish Creek. It didn't last, but in 1802 a second Catfish Baptist Church opened, with a congregation of eight men and three women, according to the Dillon County historian Durwood Stokes. Services are still held there today.

Joe sings in the choir in the church that is his family's church, almost literally. Spring Grove Baptist is a brick sanctuary at a fork in the road in the country outside Latta. The present-day chapel is the second built on land deeded to the congregation by Minnie Lane, Joe's great-great-grandmother. But the congregation began holding services a lot earlier, back in the slave days. The members built a brush arbor, a basic outdoor, open-sided shelter of timber and saplings that was not much more than a lean-to, along the basic design of a canopy today. The pews were simple wood benches.

The brush arbor was the traditional beginning of a lot of country churches in the region, put up at first sometimes to hold revivals after the harvest. It was also a sanctuary of necessity for landless slaves, off in the fields. The Spring Grove congregation's first chapel was a tiny wood meeting room no bigger than a porch, a praise house built in "back in the woods," Joe remembers being told. Those pews, too, were simple wood benches and might have been brought over or refurbished from the arbor pews.

Praise houses are a West African slave tradition more closely identified with the Gullah culture of the lowcountry, simple sanctuaries where services were held that included singing to intricate hand-clapping rhythms and sometimes dancing ritually in circles as the hymns were sung. Called shouts, they are thought to hark back to West African communal traditions and still take place in some locations. Just one of the intricacies of the service: Legs don't cross during the dancing.

Brush arbors date back to the 1700s, as far as the record suggests. But if you have been caught in weather away from housing you know exactly what they are, and they are ageless. As worship places, the arbors recall the days of white circuit preachers like the Methodist's Francis Asbury, who rode throughout the region to conduct weeklong revivals called camp meetings among remote farmers. The revivals prompted congregations and eventually churches at the meeting sites. In a few places, such as Dorchester County near Charleston, the custom has been carried on now for nearly three centuries, and among both white and black congregations. "Camps" of woodboard tents are set out in a ring, each tent owned and maintained by an individual family, where they will spend all or part of the week and often sleep on simple cots or wood bunks. Extended family return sometimes from across the country for the meeting, which has become a mix of prayer, reunion, and good eating cooked up on primitive wood-fired

The Bethea cotton press on the road into Latta. Courtesy of Cathy Petersen.

stoves. It says something about the familial nature of the meetings that they also have a long history as courting grounds. The centerpiece of a camp meeting, in the middle of the field ringed by the tents, is the tabernacle, an open-air setting of pews and a pulpit. It's a brush arbor.

That's tradition.

———

To get to Latta from I-95 you take a two-lane road, turn onto another two-lane road, and veer off through the fields. One of the first things that will catch your eye is a tall wood contraption that looks like a pagoda or an oil derrick. It's a cotton press built in 1798, "thought to be the oldest in existence," according to its historical marker. John Bethea III, one of those founding-father names in Latta, built the press. It stands today on property owned by one of his descendants.

The device and the tradition it represents tell you a lot about what would happen to Joe Williams. The long, dangling arms would have been tied to mules that plodded around the pillar in circles tightening a screw.

Born to a tenant farm worker, taken in by a crippled white farmer in the turbulent 1960s, Joe went on to farm more land singlehandedly than most other growers in the region would dare try, all the while holding down a full-time job. He made his own way through the planting seasons, pushing back at crop allotments and moneylending practices torqued against him, in the years of what became known as the black farm loan scandal. The press sits out along the roadway in front of a countryside farm near a line of planted pines, out by itself, strangely and strikingly out of place.

That sense of displacement pervades the town right down to its name. "Latta" isn't a Revolutionary War hero or a hometown cotton magnate. When the railroad tracks came through and the station was staked in 1888 for the Florence "Short Cut" line, the place became a loading station for the town of Dillon, a few miles away. It was a designed town, planned street by street in a grid from the tracks, like a lot of the Carolinas railroad towns. With the local shirts fussing over which of them the place would be named for, the railroad people couldn't quite figure out what to do. So they named it after Robert Latta, the surveyor who laid out the right of way. He came from York, on the other side of the state.

Joe lives in a country community outside Latta, a place called Temperance Hill, farm fields right down to the roadside, where homes sit in small groves of pecan. Strangers named it, too. T. C. Powers told Joe the story when Powers was about ninety years old and still ran his old country store in Temperance Hill. How it goes is that back in the late 1800s, in Scipio Williams's time, a group of people came through on horse and wagon. They decided to camp on a slight rise for the night and went looking for corn liquor. One of the places where they stopped to ask was Powers's daddy's home. They evidently were pretty intimidating, because while Powers's daddy told them no, he didn't have any liquor, he did offer some homemade wine. That apparently didn't cut it. The wagons pulled out the next day, leaving behind a sign that read "Temperance." So, people started calling the rise Temperance Hill.

"That's what Mr. Powers told me, and he was an old fellow. He'd have been about a hundred if he was still living. He used to run an old country store, and that old country store is still standing."

———

WEALTH IN THE SOUTH has an almost mythical association with land. It dates back to the antebellum glory days of white-gloved gentlemen riding off to their fields, when almost all the money was rooted in tillable acres. But it has tendriled all the way into the suburban world. A man is still considered to be in a real fix if he is land poor—owns plenty of acres but can't make money on them and doesn't have the money to keep them up. Land is the cure-all for what ails your pocketbook. In South Carolina in 2010, more than 13 million acres were in forest, nearly two-thirds of it in family hands. A lot of those acres were stands of pine, let sit for the years until the money jar gets low and they can be harvested like cracking open a piggy bank.

Owning land has been preached down through country generations like religion. Even relatively urban people of Joe's age—doctorate-educated professionals—turned around and bought country tracts to hunt, fish, farm, or fawn on just as soon as they established themselves. Land is who you are.

Scipio Williams had an eleven-horse farm. That's the way Joe heard it, three horses to a hundred acres, so his great-great-grandfather owned nearly four hundred acres. Scipio had seventeen children and left them each $800. In those days, that was worth about $80,000 apiece today, Joe was told. For a freedman family in the days after the Civil War, in the Pee Dee of South Carolina, the fortune would be singular. That was the story Joe heard as a preteen, sitting with his Granddaddy Fred by that heater on a cold night in 1967.

"Son, right down the road there is your great-great-granddaddy's land," Fred Williams began, and told about the big old plantation house that put Joe in mind of columned manors on the farms where he, his siblings, and his mother worked. Scipio built it by hand, working mostly in the winter when there were no crops in the ground. Put it together with pegs, something that awes Joe a bit to this day. The house had eight fireplaces—staggering to a child holding his hands out to a heater. And Fred told Joe the family lore about how Scipio Williams buried money somewhere on the land.

"That's what my granddaddy told me about it. I don't know. He had a great big old plantation house on the farm, and they tore it down about fifteen, twenty years ago. And I wished to the Lord—I had a chance to buy it and a lot. And if I had bought it I never would have tore the house down. Not if it burned down."

Joe calls the old homestead a peg-and-stile house. That's a curiosity. The style was a custom of homebuilding in the 1600s and 1700s, when the country was a far more rural and hands-on place. It's also called stile-and-rail, and today it's associated more with building doors. The big bracing timbers, the rafters and beams, are held together by wooden pegs called tree nails. Today you would call them trunnels. Pegs also hold the mortises and joists for the walls and doors. The panels they frame often "float" in a groove rather than being nailed in. That leaves room for them to expand and contract as the weather calls for it.

Peg houses have become one of those folk legends, said to have been built entirely without using iron nails. Joseph Dorsi, in *Architecture of American Homes*, rejects that as a myth. Nails were almost certainly used for the fine points of fastening, such a roof shingles.

But nails cost money, and a woodworker would work around that. The striking thing about a peg-and-stile house is that it's put together essentially as you would make a dresser or a coffin. It is one huge piece of furniture, a sort of masterwork for that kind of craftsman.

———

THE WAY JOE HEARD IT, Scipio kept three head of mule in stalls he built behind the house, back where he could keep an eye on them. Joe saw the old homestead house when he was growing up, down the road a way from where he lived. His mother would remark on it while passing by.

"I guess that old body worked whether he found the mules in the snow or the dirt," says Geraldine, his mom. Geraldine saw a photograph of Scipio when she was younger and was struck by just how good-looking he was. Scipio could build anything; he was a sensible man, she says. Farms in those days were always subsistence as well as business, and Scipio always put food on the table for his children, clothes on their backs, she says.

"Weren't no Southern black people. They didn't sleep in no raggedy house and things. Scipio William's children had a nice house. Grandpa Albert's children had a nice house. They didn't have to suffer the rain and stuff and have a few chickens under the house." Geraldine calls Scipio's manor a "big ole upstairs, a big ol' high tall house." It caught her imagination as well as her eye, and she made a point of riding by it often to gaze. "People would tell me that's my ol' great-granddaddy's place. I would wonder why people would give it away for syrup."

The old house with its tall wooden shutters was torn down in 1979. The syrup is another story, one that's curled up in a thick file of letters from the Scipio Williams estate.

————

GREAT-GRANDDAD ALBERT WILLIAMS took his money from the estate and started buying the land around him. Aunt Lou Williams, his sister, used to say he was so stingy that he fed his brothers and sisters flour mixed with kerosene to make it go farther. She could taste it in the bread.

"Might have tasted kerosene in their mouths, but they didn't go hungry," Geraldine says. Albert also gathered his children every day to pray.

Albert could pick a bale of cotton a day, by himself, and would do it after a day's work. The family says that he worked so hard that, if he had lived, half of Temperance Hill would have belonged to him. He died at forty-five years of age. He took wet underwear off the clothesline one Sunday morning to go to church, left it on all day, and died of pneumonia.

His widow married a preacher and "sold [some of] her land to the white people," Geraldine says.

Granddad Fred grew "tobacco so pretty" and "cotton like snow in the field." Geraldine remembers she and her siblings had to pick twelve bales of cotton before they could go to school. Fred was a well digger, and a good one. He used a grape vine as a divining rod and never put down a well that didn't have water. He bored the well with a wooden mallet. Fred "threw all his wealth away on liquor and women," in Geraldine's words. Now he had eleven-year-old Joe in front of the space heater. He told him he wished he'd done differently.

"I told him, 'Grandpa, I wished the land was still here, in the family.' And he said, 'Well, it would have been good, son. But they sold it out, one thing to another'n.'"

————

JOE BARELY KNOWS his father. He sees him at choir practice in the church. When they go by each other in town, the man won't acknowledge him unless Joe greets him first. Some years back, the man gave Joe and his twin sister,

Judy, $50 each after his mother told the man he never gave them anything special. $50.

"Child support," Joe says, spitting out the words.

———

JOE EYES THE FOR SALE SIGN on a disused farm next to his great-great-grandfather's former holdings. In his mind he's not done buying land. But they want too much, $4,000 an acre, for land well up from the silts of the Pee Dee.

Chapter 2

Brick Bats

JOE LIVES IN THE WHITE CLAPBOARD country house of the people who took him in. The handrail up the concrete steps to the pantry door is made from steel plumbing pipe. The brick foundation has cracks. The roof has the rumpled look of a weathered hat, and the window blinds sag in the middle like an old man's smile.

This is the Copeland Moody house. There's a used-up refrigerator in the back yard under the live oak and pecan, a brick fireplace, a stone bench with a planter on it. And there's an old shed that's boarded shut except for the window, where you can reach in to grab the tools leaning against its sill.

Moody was a farmer who owned a fertilizer warehouse in Latta. The warehouse, the Moody farm—with its long dirt road through the fields of his seventy-five acres, the sand drive up to the house all pebbled and looking like a shelled beach—made the family rich people in the eyes of the kids around Temperance Hill. They worked for Moody in the fields around his house.

The shed is a 1950s-era, hammered-together, aluminum-siding travel trailer, with half-moon saw cuts for the wheels well ajar from the ground, like the open mouths of nestling birds. It's one room, no bigger than the old car it was built to be towed behind. It sits up on brick bats, crumbled pieces of brick. It's full of debris and old tools. Inside, there's a disused metal counter the size of a shelf against one wall, with a jerry-rigged sink that drains out the wall.

Joe moved to Copeland Moody's farm when he was thirteen years old, and the shed is where he lived. They ran a cord from the house to the shed window to power a space heater.

The shed now is crumpled and coming apart. It's not tied down, and it has never budged. It stood up to the ripping winds of Hurricane Hugo in 1989 and didn't move an inch, even though the storm blew over a storage building alongside. And that building was tied down. "Ain't that something?" Joe says with pride. There's an aluminum chair alongside where you can sit a while if you want.

"Me and Jimmy Moody put it here in '68. Hurricane Hugo come through here. Other hurricanes come through here. It's sitting on the blocks where it's sitting just like you see it sitting and never moved."

More revealing, Joe has never moved it, even though it's now falling in and does no more than hold a few tools you could just as easily lean up against the wall inside the pantry door to the home place. He just likes holding onto it, he says. It's a point of pride.

"That's where I lived. Right there. Right there. I didn't have no running water. I didn't have no bathroom. I go by there and brush my teeth." And he points to the hose running from the white house he now owns.

County staffers knocked on the door to the house a few years back. They were naming all the private-use roads in the country to keep emergency medical crews responding to 911 calls from fumbling from one dirt drive to another to find people who could describe their place only by their family name. The county wanted to call the long dirt stretch down to Joe's place "Williams Road." Joe said no. The street sign says Copeland Moody Road. It's a testament to Joe's loyalty to the man who took him in as a field-hand kid and taught him how to farm. Copeland Moody bought the land in the 1940s, Joe says. It was always Copeland's farm to him, even after the Moodys held an auction in 1970 and sold the farmland around the house to pay for Copeland's medical bills.

"This is the old homeplace right here. Where I was raised. This is where I started out at, right here. I moved here in September of '68."

———

COPELAND MOODY had a big face with big ears, piercing sad eyes behind thick horn-rimmed glasses. He looked like he lived, in pain. He had rheumatoid arthritis. He was on crutches by the time Joe went to live and work on his farm.

How it happened was Geraldine sent Joe down the road to the store to fetch her some Winston cigarettes and Grandmom some Peach Sweet snuff. The errand was worth a dime to Joe, and a dime meant a handful of two-for-a-penny sugar wafer cookies. You could see the Bass farm across the road from Granddad's house, and Joe had been watching a man planting soybeans. Jimmy Moody was twenty years old, the tallest of the Moody boys, Joe says. It was his first planting on his own, off the family farm.

Jimmy is the child most like his father, they say—friendly, the sort of man who talked eye to eye with the day workers he hired. People like him. In his early 60s, Jimmy has that gentle smile in his eye of a kind man and the burly body of a working man. He drives up to meet you in an old pickup truck with the roots of a pulled stump sticking up from the bed. He's dressed in clean clothes and dirty work boots. He and Joe are blood brothers, a story in itself.

Jimmy was trying to get the planting done. A helper was out sowing seeds in the field from an International diesel tractor with tricycle wheels. Jimmy was turning the seeds in a barrel in the bed of his red '56 Ford pickup. When this little kid came up.

"I asked him questions, a lot of questions. Who you? What's your name? Where you from? Is this your farm?"

Here Jimmy was trying to get beans planted and this ten-year-old tenant worker kid was pestering the heck out of him. But oddly, they hit it off, he and this black kid half his age.

"Joe was aggravating. But he was persistent. He's always been persistent. And he was personable."

Joe kept coming around, and Jimmy kept finding him things to do, to keep him from asking questions if nothing else. Joe talked all the time. He talked about owning the farmland he was working on.

Then Joe's mother moved to a tenant shack in the pines at the edge of a nearby farm. The old shack was rough, particularly for a woman with a flock of children. The front porch stood high enough off the ground that you could look beneath and see there was no underpinning. In hurricane country, underpinning is everything if you want the place you're sheltered in to stay put in a storm. One of the ways to tell a good contractor is by just how many ties he wants to make. The shack was missing some of the pine board siding and some of the window glass. A small woodpile out back was all that supplied heat for the household.

"One of the things that sticks in my mind," Jimmy recalls, "Joe had a little brother, he was standing on the front porch naked as a jaybird, and it was wintertime, peeing off the side of the porch. That's just the way life was."

Mother and children began working for Jimmy, and he began stopping by the shack in the morning to pick up Joe on his way to the fields. The more Jimmy gave Joe to do, the more Joe wanted to do. In the field he wanted to do it all. Most of all, Joe wanted to drive the tractor.

"Boy, he did," Jimmy says. Joe didn't let it go. He was at Jimmy so persistently that Jimmy put him up in the seat alongside him, letting him take the wheel a while, then teaching a maneuver at a time. Joe would pump the diesel fuel, do some drags down a field, simple mechanics. It says something about Joe that the first "public" job he talked his way into, at nine years old, was pumping gas at a general store down the road toward Latta.

"Wherever the gasoline was, that's where Joe wanted to be," Jimmy says. "I used to tell him I was going to get a baby thumb [pacifier], fill it full of diesel fuel, and hang it around his neck."

Sure enough, Joe found his way to the Yazoo 246 push mower—"one of the best mowers ever built," he says now—and began cutting the grass at the Moody farm. By that time, Copeland Moody had gotten to the point where his hands were drawn up and not much use. He had had a lot of surgery.

"I'd never known him to walk the way you and I walk," Joe says.

Copeland would drive up in his big red Ford pickup looking to help Jimmy, to do the running around errands because he couldn't do much more. The pain had become crippling. Joe began riding with Copeland to the warehouse, where he'd pick up a broom and sweep. The one thing a workingman likes to see is a man who likes to work.

"Yeah, he smoothed Daddy over in a short while," Jimmy said.

————

Riding with Copeland Moody was a participatory sport. Abruptly the truck would jerk to the side of the road: Copeland had spotted a cold drink bottle. Recyclable.

"Here, boy, get out of the car, boy. Git. Git. Git. Git," Joe mimics. "Ten cents, boy." The bottle got tossed on the pile of bottles in a crate in the pickup truck bed.

"He'd see those bottles a half-mile down the road," Jimmy says, only partly joking.

Copeland Moody was a churchgoing man, hobbling his way into Ebenezer Southern Methodist Church each Sunday—which incongruously sat just down the road from Scipio Williams's old land—where he sang in the choir.

"I cannot spell 'can't,'" Copeland would say over and over. "I can't spell that, Joe."

Copeland lived through the Great Depression, lived through World War II. He knew the difference between need and want. The kids got away with nothing. There would be plenty of food on the table, but you didn't get up from your plate with any left. He worked Jimmy and Joe to the bone—"He worked me like a barred mule put up wet," Joe says. Joe tells a great story about laying out of school and working hard all week with the spreader in the fields. He wanted a little money, and he found Copeland shaving in the bathroom. He asked him for a dollar so he could go get a haircut. Copeland couldn't get his arthritic hand in his pants pocket, so he kept change in his shirt pocket.

"He reached in his pocket and said, 'Here's fifty cents,'" Joe recalls. That's what a haircut cost, fifty cents. "I didn't say a word. I just took it and went about my business."

Copeland would tell Jimmy over and over, "Son, a poor man ain't got nothing but his word. When he loses that, he loses everything." It was one of those dad-things that stuck. Jimmy considers it the common denominator of the people he knows of his dad's generation. It's lost now, he says. "I don't see it anywhere. I don't see it in business. I don't see it in the media. I don't see it in schools."

When Joe is angry his voice will drop to a mutter and he'll cuss under his breath. Copeland didn't cuss and didn't abide by it. If he heard one of his children or Joe cuss, he'd give him back something to think about. One time he caught Joe cussing up a storm at a highboy tractor. "Boy, you're going to hell," Copeland said. "You're going straight to hell. You're not going to stop along the way."

"He had a temper, but he was normally an easygoing man. He loved to work, but he loved to see people work more than he loved to work," Jimmy says with a wry grin.

Joe was just prickly enough to get along with Copeland Moody.

"He'd always want to tell me what to do, and I'd tell him sometimes it ain't gonna work that way. And he'd tell me, 'You hush. It's going to work this way.' And then it wouldn't work."

———

For all the decorous good manners of the region, to be welcomed into a white person's home was a rare thing for a black person in the country back then. Jimmy didn't think anything of it when Copeland drove up and told them there was some dinner waiting for the two of them at the house. Joe did. He had never been before. The year was 1966.

He and Jimmy were unloading liquid nitrogen tanks for sale display in the Moody warehouse, Moody Agri Co., when Jimmy said, "Let's go and get some dinner." They hopped in the truck and drove to the farmhouse with Joe's mind racing. The meal was fried fish and cornbread, slaw, and iced tea if you wanted. For Jimmy it was nothing special: Daddy told them to go eat and that's what they did. Jimmy remembers mostly that Joe didn't drink much tea. Joe liked Kool-Aid, the sugary flavored drink. But when a pitcher of red Kool-Aid was set in front of him he didn't know what it was. He had had only grape Kool-Aid. He didn't know there were other flavors.

Neither of them thought much about the fact that Jimmy ate at the kitchen table and Joe ate sitting on a stool at the chest-high freezer in the utility room.

———

IT WAS FUNNY TIMES for tenant farming in South Carolina, a life stuck on traditions and habit. And place. Just a few years earlier, one man in Latta had tried to take a stool at the drink counter in the drugstore. The owner threw him out, then threw the seats out to make sure it wouldn't happen again. That was 1963, and Joe was nine years old. In 1965 Martin Luther King Jr. led the mass protest march in Selma, a defining moment in the civil rights struggle.

"When Martin Luther King marched on Selma, Alabama," Joe will say, nodding his head, things changed. In just a few more years, three students would be shot dead and a few dozen injured in the Orangeburg Massacre just down the road from Latta, when police opened fire on a protest outside a segregated bowling alley near South Carolina State University. That would be 1968, and there isn't a whole lot of need to talk about what else happened that year. It shook through Latta the way it reverberated everywhere else in the South. Joe remembers knocking on the front door of one of the nicer homes in Latta at Thanksgiving in 1965—remembers the season and the year precisely—to ask if the family needed the yard raked. The woman who answered told him if he knocked on her door again she would call the law.

Just a year or two before Joe moved in with the Moodys, he was walking home from seeing teen star Frankie Avalon in the movies—where he sat in the black balcony—with some friends and his little sisters. The segregated balcony was salt in what had become an open sore in the town. Joe will tell you straight up that some kids sitting in that balcony tossed ice and cigarette butts into the theater below. They were walking home that time and a '55 Oldsmobile full of older kids shot by, stopped abruptly, and backed up. Nobody waited to see what that was about. They scattered, and the joke later was that Truman, one of his friends, ran thirty-five miles an hour that night.

———

QUEEN GORDON, Joe's cousin, would come down from Pennsylvania two or three times per year to visit family while she was growing up in the 1960s. Her cousins would tell her she didn't know how easy she had it up north.

She is an ardent, straightforward woman with a soft-featured face and discerning eyes. At the time, race relations in Pennsylvania were as "theirs and ours" as anywhere else. And sure, she had heard the stories. Her father's brother had been hanged in a small North Carolina tobacco town in the 1920s, the body left dangling for a couple of days in the town square. But the smack of segregation in the Pee Dee stunned her.

"It's hard for me to understand why, why people are so vicious to each other," she says a half-century later.

In Pennsylvania, you could walk into the five-and-dime store to get a cold drink. You couldn't sit at the counter to drink it, but you could get it and take it outside. In South Carolina, "maybe they would give it to you and maybe they wouldn't," Queen said. "You had to put your money down. You couldn't hand it to them. They didn't want to touch you." The first time she got her ticket at the movie theater, she started to walk in and was stopped. She got very outspoken, in her words. "They were ready to call the cops," she said. Her uncle grabbed her, pulled her away, and brought her around to the back, where she stepped up to the unlit recess of a small balcony that wasn't any more than a raised floor in the dark.

"We sat on cinderblocks," she says, her voice astonished and exasperated a half-century later, "those big gray cinderblocks. I don't even remember what the movie was about, because it was dark, dusty, and those gray cinderblocks. We sat on cinderblocks. I had never heard of such a thing. There was an outhouse out back, and oh God, it was nasty."

ALL THIS WAS GOING ON. White bathrooms and colored bathrooms. The white restaurant in downtown Latta where blacks were served by black help through a window in the back. Prejudice was a way of life. The races didn't mix.

"It wasn't a question," Jimmy says plainly. "What Joe and I found was an area we could mix in, develop a friendship and a mutual relationship that didn't have those pressures." They found it in the crop rows.

When Joe agreed to move in, he had a straight-up talk with Copeland, saying he wouldn't stand for being called nigger. Copeland said that if anyone used the word to "tell me and I'll get it corrected." But moving thirteen-year-old Joe onto the farm, with its echoes of sharecropper and slavery, got people talking—not so much in the Moodys' community, where it wasn't much more than another makeshift tenant farming arrangement. The talk was in Joe's community.

"It was tough for me going to school, one of the black-dominant schools, you get picked at a lot. It wasn't no easy test, wasn't no easy road, no easy test at all." He was called "the colored Moody," "white man's boy," the Moodys' slave, or worse.

That figures, to no small extent, but Jimmy says there was something more to it than that. There was Joe.

"Joe never presented himself as something other than what he was"—a poor kid who wanted to learn how to farm. Jimmy walked away from the slurs. "I wouldn't give them the time of day." Joe ignored it, too, when he could, in what would become almost a mantra for his life. "Naw, naw. You let it go," he says. "I've seen a lot of things. I heard a lot of things said about the color of my skin. I just keep walking."

It's like him that the thing he remembers precisely about that night after the movies is that car was an Oldsmobile, a '55 Oldsmobile. But the mouths got to him.

"A black coming along and living with a white family back then, you're going to school with a lot of kids, and some of them have big mouths. Sometimes you've got to fistfight and hit people in the mouths, you know what I mean. Pickin'. Pickin'. I never attacked, I wouldn't pick at nobody. But I wouldn't let nobody pick at me, so it was kind of tough times. But some of those same guys who had their mouths pickin', they had to come work on my farm. They had so much mouth, some of those same guys shucked tobacco for me, see what I'm talking about?"

Joe used to think about it when he was writing those checks for the work, thinking he would sign it "Geraldine's bastard child."

"I didn't do it," he says, "but I thought about it."

Chapter 3

Aunt Lou

THE SLAVE NAME SCIPIO is ringed with ironies. Scipio was a Roman general who lived about a century before Christ. He is noted largely for his pride, something that maddened his enemies.

Scipio conquered a large stretch of land in Spain and wanted Africa. Denied the money to do it, he conquered land in Sicily with a volunteer army and won the money to cross the Mediterranean. He conquered Africa, defeated the legendary Hannibal when Hannibal tried to make peace. Scipio was no weenie.

He was called Scipio Africanus after the land he conquered. So the name Scipio became an unusual but not unheard-of name for a slave, as a kind of historical in-joke for classically educated owners. The name shows up several times in nineteenth-century census rolls for South Carolina. The 1880 census that lists Scipio as a forty-three-or-so-year-old also lists a twelve-year-old Scipio Williams, apparently not related, not too far away in the McMillans community near Mullins in Marion County.

―――――

"ONE BOX and two sacks." That was the listed possessions of one slave in a nineteenth-century account of sale of brood or chattel of James Lane. Shirley Cribb Matlock, a cousin of Joe, includes the account in "Lane Family/The Dark Side . . . The House that Jack Built," a genealogy of Joe's forbearers along with the Williams. Her research led to a rapprochement between the black and white Lane families.

"One churn and a lot of sacks" read the next one.

―――――

CHARLES LANE IS GENIAL, with an easy drawl of a voice. He is genuinely friendly to a stranger. He keeps a BB gun instead of a .22 out on the porch leaning up against the frame of his kitchen door to run off whatever comes up, raccoons, dogs. His folks were friends with the Moodys when Joe came to live with them.

"And then there was Joe," Charles says with that drawl. "He come up. The last child." Both of them get to laughing. "Come up out of the wilderness," Joe says. The two of them are about the same age and as teens became lifelong friends. Coincidentally, because of the ties between the two Lane families, Charles and Joe are also cousins, something neither realized at the time.

———

THE FARM WHERE Joe's mom was tenanted used to belong to Scipio Williams. Joe drives his little blue pickup truck past a field lot holding a modest brick house, the place where Scipio's peg-built farmhouse used to stand, and points it out. He calls Scipio "Grandpa." Then he drives down the road to another farm, where his great-great-grandfather was raised. By a white man.

Scipio Williams was brought up by a doctor who lived in one of those old manor homes, back up on a hill outside Latta. The hill is wooded now, another home is set farther back, and there's a light pole where the manor used to stand. Joe heard the story as an adult; it was told to him by a descendant in the family. Raised by a white man! The notion floored him. All the stories told in his family about Scipio Williams, all those years with the Moodys, nobody had mentioned that.

"You know, how that thing turns, it's just amazing. You know what I'm trying to say to you?"

Clement "Olin" Epps lives in a home he built himself, just like his dad did in 1910. He's older now, walks crookedly, and clutches the rail as he climbs the brick steps to his home. But when the visit is over, he's headed back to the barn. He has work to do. He wears paint-streaked Dickie's overalls and moccasins. His fingers fret with a paper card as he talks.

Epps was a school principal, one of a number of teachers and school officials around town that Joe became friends with after he graduated. As he got to know the Epps family he heard about his great-great-grandfather from a relative. Epps's granddaddy raised Scipio Williams. His name was Francis or Franklin Marion Monroe; when you look at the old papers you see it both ways. Monroe was a doctor, evidently well-to-do enough to own slaves. Epps's aunt, who grew up in the Monroe household, used to talk about Scipio all the time, another relative told Joe. But Clement Epps doesn't recall much talk in his family about Scipio. That was then.

By the time Joe graduated, his situation had become a familiar one among local educators. They all talk, in one fashion or another, about his pluck.

"If Joe told you something, it was the truth," Epps says. "And he kept his mouth shut. He didn't bother anybody that I know of. You know, there's some students that when they come in, they come in just to stir problems, be mean and everything else. This one really didn't cause any trouble. He didn't start any trouble."

House building seems to run in the Monroe family and maybe partly provided for Scipio's carpentry talent. Monroe's old house burned the Sunday after Pearl Harbor. The family built a bigger house on the site, back under a cope of hardwood in the fields, and Epps's daughter lives there now. Joe would like to set up Little Joe in that house, one more tag to the heritage.

———

MOST OF WHAT the Williams family knows about Scipio is what they remember being told by Catherine Tuluder Williams, familiarly called Aunt Lula and known by her family as Aunt Lou, or Lu. She was Scipio's sixth child. After his death, in 1904, she took custody of the four youngest children and lived in her late father's house until she sold it, in 1920.

In her later years, she ironed for a white family, incongruously also named Williams but apparently not related by blood or title, and did it until she was a hundred years old. Joe remembers them mostly by the car they drove when they came by to pick her up for work—"a white '57 Chevrolet, red interior." She taught Sunday school at Andrews Chapel until shortly before she died.

In a flashpan photo taken when she was young, Lou stares slight down and off to one side, maybe a little frightened by the bright pop. Her eyes are pensive, and she has the serious air of a tutored student. She told the family that all of Scipio Williams's children were educated. Joe heard that Scipio hired a teacher to come to the farm.

In *A History of Marion County* written in 1890, W. W. Sellers noted that the town had a population of 467 and, remarking on its advancements, says, "There are two or three colored churches, of moderate pretensions, gone up." Sellers also noted there was a "colored graded school" and added that school properly is taught in a building separate from whites.

Scipio might well have hired the teacher.

In a family photo from her later years, Lou stares up from a chair where she is apparently reading from the tattered family Bible. She has the piercing eyes of someone who looks right through you and knows exactly who you are. By then she lived just outside the heart of town in a house in the shade of a big pecan tree. She still slept on the bed her father made. "My poppa made these dressers," she would tell Joe.

"She did not depend on anyone, no one. She raised chickens; she had eggs. She was very strong. And that is why the Williams females are so strong," said Queen Gordon, Joe's cousin. Queen spent time with Aunt Lou as a teen, coming down from Pennsylvania each year for the Fourth of July holiday and then back again in the fall for the thick, sweet molasses tradition of sugar-cane cutting.

"Sugar cane to me was like a piece of wood," Queen said. "She showed me how to strip it and eat it. She said, 'You don't chew it. You suck on it.'"

Aunt Lou became a mentor of sorts to Queen, who would find herself in conversations getting schooled about world events such as slave times, the Second World War, or the ongoing integration struggles. When the hardcore segregation moods and practices Queen encountered in South Carolina outraged her enough, she would vent to Aunt Lou, and Aunt Lou would tell her, "Baby, it'll get better."

"She was without a doubt the most generous, kindest, smartest woman I have ever met," Queen said. "She was just a sweet one."

At one hundred years old, Aunt Lou still threaded sewing needles without her glasses. She still walked from her side-street home the few blocks to the C&S Grocery. She would do it on Friday, to get the fixings for a big Saturday dinner when the family visited or for occasions. Workers in the store would take her home with the groceries. Geraldine, among other family, would come shuck the peas and beans. She recalls having her birthday dinner at the house. Lou kept a vegetable garden, did her own housekeeping, laundry, and cooking. She loved flowers and kept a border of orange marigolds around the front porch. Alongside she grew catnip, which she made into a tea to treat fevers, and mullet, or rape, a winter green that tastes like collards.

Her home was a timepiece. Along with the dressers, a china closet, chairs, and a chest her father made, she kept a purple-hued crystal goblet with her mother's name, Laura, etched into it along with the date 1897. It was a gift Scipio brought home for his wife from a fair. Queen Gordon was enamored of the goblet on her visits. It was the first time she had seen words etched in glass. Aunt Lou kept her mother's wicker fan on the wall, a showpiece fancy of the times.

Scipio "was a tailor, he made clothes for the white people," she told a *Florence Morning Star* interviewer on her 104th birthday. He farmed and he built coffins. As a child, she picked cotton and pulled fodder but didn't plow. "I had too many brothers to do that," she said. She recalled the great 1886 Charleston earthquake. "The house was just a-shakin' and a-reelin' and a-rockin'. We didn't know enough to be scared." That she didn't remember any major damage to Scipio's peg-built home is itself a mark of his craftsmanship. Even at 104, she had a clear, strong voice, and she loved to talk, as the interviewer noted. Asked why she had lived such a long life, she said, "I don't know. I serve the Lord and I never hurt nobody. I pray to the Lord."

Aunt Lou had a wood stove but stoked her fireplace for heat. She did her cooking—all her cooking—with an iron skillet on a two-burner electric hot plate. Queen can still taste the ho' cakes. Lou kept a set of pots so old there were holes in the bottoms. She would have Geraldine over to put metal patches over the holes.

"Stingy, good God, she was stingy," Geraldine says with a smile in her eye, remembering.

Lou kept her chicken pen behind the house, where you couldn't see it from the road, and swept her yard clean so that you wouldn't know there were chickens. She could cook up a storm, usually the chickens. When they got loose from the pen, Joe used to run them down for her. He could earn a little change cutting firewood for her. A little change.

"She was a little tight," Joe says with wistful smile. "Cut and tow it to the house. I'd take that ten cents and say, 'Thank you, Ma'am.'"

As an adult Aunt Lou was rarely if ever bedridden, except for one visit to the hospital. At 101 she began using a cane. Joe remembers stopping by when she sat on her porch at 103 years old to ask how she was.

"I'm all right today, boy," she would say. She lived on her own until she died, in 1976, at 105 years old, of pneumonia. Lou was a spinster. She told the *Morning Star* interviewer she had had two suitors, who died in a flu epidemic. She told Joe's family a different story.

"Never been married once. Never had a man," Joe says. "The man she loved got killed in a saw mill."

———

SINCE LOU'S DEATH, Scipio's story has become one of those family memories told and retold until it has misted into lore if not legend.

"He and Grandma Minnie used to get on the train. And one of those people [Lincoln] used to meet in the kitchen, one of those people was my

great-grandpa, Scipio Williams. All he could do, he was what was called a coun-
cilman for the colored race back then. He could not say nothing to the white
race of people, to try to make it better for the colored race of people. 'Cause
Lincoln freed the slaves. And right after he freed the slaves he got killed. John
Booth shot him."

————

PICKING COTTON is hot, nasty, buggy, bent-over work. Hour after hour.

"Bad on the hands. Back breaking. The cotton balls, when they break open,
they've got small little thorns on them," says George Legette, Joe's childhood
friend from Temperance Hill. "Sometimes you'd be bending over. Sometimes
you'd get on your knees and crawl."

And if the thorns weren't bad enough, cotton worms cling to the under-
side of leaves, out of sight. The worms, really moth caterpillars, have bristling
hairs that secrete venom wicked enough to leave rashes and sometimes scars.
In the fields they are called stinging worms, because there's also cutworms,
cornworms, Southern armyworms, and so on. They make up a sort of mix-and-
match set of various moth larvae, and field workers tended to use the names
indiscriminately. The worms are related to the boll weevil, and infestations
could do a lot of damage to the leaves of a crop.

"It was so hot," recalls Earlene McKay, Joe's older sister. "And you would be
glad to see night come." But in the countryside of Dillon and Marion Counties,
there weren't a lot of other opportunities. When Jimmy Moody went to collect
field help, workers would run down the already-loaded truck as it drove off, grab
hold, and jam themselves aboard.

"I'd have to get out and tell them and tell them to get off," Jimmy recalls.

————

He's not from Philadelphia. He's from Latta, as much cotton as he's
picked down here.

    Joe, about a popular entertainer

JOE'S MOTHER put him in the field with Judy when they were four years old. He
and his mother will both tell you that. He grew up working, he says. His siblings
were all field hands on a large spread that felt like a plantation, Joe recalls. In one
of those odd turnabouts in life, the overseers later became sharecroppers and
now rent the land as farmers. Today, they are Joe's friends.

"I picked one side of the cotton row, and Judy picked the other side. Earlene, my older sister, was over there on the other cotton row with my momma. We had a twenty-five-pound of flour sack tied to us that we took. We were too small to have a regular cotton sack. Me and Judy would pick eighty pounds of cotton together, a day together, that's what we would pick."

Their cotton sacks were burlap flour sacks with a strip of old dungarees as a tie, because the kids were too small to drag along that full-size sack. You'd take a pair of dungarees, cut a cord from it, cut a hole in the sack, and sling it over your neck to one side, depending on whether you were left- or right-handed. A cotton boll weighs about a tenth of an ounce, meaning there were about 160 to a pound. You were paid $3 per hundred pounds picked. Adults would carry as much as two hundred pounds of cotton in a sack.

Even compared to other farm work, cotton picking was relentless and grueling—and any kind of farm labor at the time could be brutal. Joe recalls as a young child watching a man work two mules in the heat of the day. The mules were so old their teeth were falling out, so poorly fed you could count their ribs. They were in a mud hole, and the man was working them hard to get them out. All of a sudden, one of the mules keeled over, taking the other one with him. Neither of them ever got back up.

"It was scary. He kicked it. That was it." Joe can still see the legs kicking in the air. "Breaking the land for tobacco." Joe says it with emphasis, shaking his head mightily. "Plowed them to death. To death. To death. Heart attacks."

Farmers liked to put women and children in the field. Women could pick more than men, sometimes three hundred pounds per day. They were better with their hands. Kids were just lower to the ground and could pick easier.

As the oldest child, Earlene felt responsible for her siblings and remembers she had to run after them all the time. Joe "wasn't so mouthy as he is now," she says with a coy grin. But the twins were born mischievous—Geraldine talks about how, after she gave birth to Joe, "I went down the elevator and there came Judy"—and a little antagonistic. Judy would scratch Joe in the face to distract him and then steal his milk. Even today they can't hang together long without fussing at each other.

The dual role of being a kid and a babysitter had its moments. One time, Earlene had Judy and Joe bury her in the dirt with her head sticking out, for fun. But once she got buried, it wasn't so fun.

"I told them to do it, and they did. Then when I got out, I whacked both of them," she said. But the family members looked out for one another. When Judy and Joe were in the playpen, Earlene would go across the road for some of her Aunt Blanche's good biscuits. And she'd bring some back for the twins. She hated children when she was growing up, Earlene says with a smile. She has five of her own now.

In the field, if Earlene didn't break up any impromptu break, Mom was quick to. "C'mon here. Don't you get to talkin'. Don't you get that cotton stuff on your tail."

But for a kid, maybe even more than an adult, cotton picking was numbingly repetitive. Any distraction would do to get your mind off it. Anything. And after a night back in the countryside without much besides your imagination for distraction, seeing somebody go streaming by in a machine took on a getaway air that was irresistible. Joe's mom never owned a car.

"Out in the country, you're so poor, you come out of the woods on the side of the road and you're just looking," Joe says. "As a kid, you just want to see everything. You'd be pickin' cotton and a car would go by. I'd want to see. I'd want to look at it. I'd want me a car. That's how things was. That's how things was." It might have been the spark for Joe's lifelong love of machinery. Dead mules or not, Joe wanted to be behind the plow from the first time he saw it move.

"I wanted to plow so bad when I was little," he says wistfully a half-century later. Too young to handle the rig, he would walk alongside holding the lines as an older kid worked the blades.

———

"ONE THING I LOVE about my momma, she come off the hip straight. I don't want sugar coating. She don't sugarcoat. I love my son, but if he weren't no good, I'd tell you he ain't no good."

Geraldine Williams sits with her legs wide apart and a quiet, settled pride to her posture. She speaks like Joe, staccato, forthright, but her voice has a weary tail to it.

"I've been sitting here waiting for my good days," she says from her chair on the porch.

She has the clouded gray eyes of age, a dignity her eyes wear as a frown. She's a little embarrassed in front of a stranger, a little reticent talking about her life. She tends to look away when she talks about something she's not comfortable with. Otherwise she peers into your eyes. She is seventy-seven years old.

"I worked hard. My children are amazed I'm living. They'll say, yeah, my momma's walking around in her garden working. I worked hard. I worked hard," she says, and her voice feints almost to a cry. "Ain't scared of working."

Geraldine Williams. Courtesy of Cathy Petersen.

She has thirty-five grandchildren, eight great-grandchildren, and three or four great-great-grandchildren. When she sits at the kitchen counter in her modest prefab house, she sits where she can see out the front door. A jumble of prescription vials sits there. Geraldine has "the sugar," diabetes.

"I don't have many friends. They think I'm so mean. But I'm the type of person to tell you what I want to tell you. And when I tell you, I tell the truth over my heart and it's gone. I don't hold no meanness on anybody. I'm going to tell you what I tell you. I'm Grandpa Albert's granddaughter."

———

GERALDINE WAS A FIELD WORKER; getting the fieldwork done meant she and the children could stay in the shack. That was life. When she was younger, going to school meant a four-mile walk through the countryside.

"She would work hard through the week and then on the weekend get nipsy, bless her heart," Joe says.

Joe was one of fourteen children she had. She worked every one. She names them one by one, and about each one she says the child was a hard worker. "They were hardworking children." And she kept them in line. If they got to cutting up in the department store aisles while she was shopping for clothes, she would snap a single clap of her hands and they got back in line.

"We were like soldiers," Joe remembers. "Geraldine tore some tail up when we were comin' up." At four years old, Joe had a job picking those forty pounds of cotton per day, and this literally helped keep the family together.

"At first he didn't pick fifty. So I whipped him. I whupped him right there." She laughs. Joe laughs, loud. "I had to work him. I had to work," she says. She didn't like to hit her kids, she said, so she would get skinny little switches to do it, almost willow thin, "like you could tie around his arm." Fifty years later, she thinks back on it, and her face visibly pains. "Joe, I didn't never bruise you up, did I? But it was hard. We had it hard."

Joe shows where the field house was on the old tenant farm, back up in the pines on a small knoll at the end of field. He's a little taken aback that nothing's there anymore but pines. It's so grown in he can't be sure exactly where the house stood. Geraldine lived with her first seven children in the house, with no husband.

"And a woman with seven kids back in those days was considered a bad woman," Joe says, with a small, sardonic draw on the word "bad." "'Germy old bastardy-looking ragged young'uns' are what some of the family members used to tell us, you know? That's what was said. Mmhm. That's exactly what was said. That ain't right."

Joe's dreams growing up were work. He wanted to drive trucks or to be an equipment manager for a pro football team. But he always came back to wanting to farm. Tractors were all Joe ever wanted to talk about, his childhood friend George Legette says. He wanted to be one of the biggest farmers around.

———

THERE'S WHEAT GROWING in the field that Great-Great-Grandaddy Scipio owned. When Joe goes to work that land, he tells his wife he's going to Granddad's place.

"This is some of Grandpa's old land, by that house here. This is some of my part, that I bought."

Chapter 4

Blood Brothers

THE SHED AT THE MOODY FARM wasn't much at all, even for a travel trailer, barely room for a cot and camp stove. The idea of living in it would make a lot of people's skin crawl. Joe was tickled.

"I had my own room, a little place, not real big, nice little bed. Real clean. You know what I mean. Just a place to myself. I could lay my stuff down, nobody was going to bother with it, you know?"

How it happened is that Copeland Moody had a twin brother. When his brother died, Copeland told Jimmy to go get his brother's trailer and bring it to the house. Jimmy took Joe along, eight miles down the road, on a hot August afternoon, in an International flatbed truck that Joe recalls to this day, right down to its color—"Red International 1965, low saw, four-speed with a red button on the side."

Joe was working with Jimmy or Copeland nearly all the time now, spending most of his days, and long days, with Jimmy farming. Jimmy recalls putting him off at his mom's tenant shack at night, and sometimes late at night. Joe was with the Moodys a lot more than he was going to school. Jimmy had talked to his dad about what Joe's life was like at the shack and about getting him through school. Copeland had spoken about Joe maybe coming to live with them.

"Daddy would talk about what a good heart he had and how he needed a chance," Jimmy recalls. Copeland and Jimmy had even discussed the legalities of taking custody of Joe. But nothing had been decided or at least acknowledged.

Copeland talked with both of them about the trailer, but all three left the biggest question unspoken. Then in August, just after Joe's thirteenth birthday, Jimmy and Joe drove out to get it, the ride an unusually quiet, unsettled one for the unlikely friends. Joe was pretty sure he knew what was going on, but it wasn't a thing you could just come out and say. Or ask. Nobody really knew what the right way to do it was.

"The main thing was for Daddy to get his trailer, that was number one," Jimmy said. Nobody really wanted to dwell on what might come next. Copeland went to talk to Geraldine.

"Yeah, it was hard with me," Geraldine says with a small tuck of her head. "It hurt me. It did hurt me real bad. It always worried me. But as the years come up I had to give it up. But it worried me. Nobody knew about it but me and the Lord, but it worried me. Had to give up my oldest son. God, I missed him. I didn't never tell anybody how bad I missed him."

There's more to the story. Joe had been a blue baby, one of those newborns who didn't get enough oxygen before birth, and for a while afterward he couldn't sit up straight. When Geraldine went into the field, she left Joe and Judy in a crib, with Aunt Blanche. Blanche tied Joe straight up in a chair to feed him so that his back would get strong. It seems to have worked. Joe became the child who stayed by Geraldine and talked to her, the one who loved the fields. Even as a grown man, he would come by on a Saturday after working all week. They would go out to the field, plant peas, and talk things over. She calls him "my oldest little boy."

The idea was she would get married, and they would get a big farm and work it together. Then Geraldine got involved with a man who turned out to be a piece of work. The money he earned went to cigarettes and drink and into the poker machine down at the store.

"Messed up my life," she says. "My husband weren't worth throwing across the river. He weren't worth killing," she says. But she married him because he asked and she had children to look out for. A field-working woman with that many children didn't have a lot of options.

"I prayed to the Lord and told Him I want a husband. I thought the Lord had sent him to me. But it was the devil." He was rough on her kids, she says, called them her bastard children and told her that his own children, with their brown skins, were going to do better than hers, with their darker skins. That was why Joe wanted to get out.

"Go where he was better treated," George Legette said.

———

GERALDINE STAYED with the man for years. She is defiantly proud of the day she walked out.

"I told him if I get the chance to leave you I'm going to leave you. So I took up and I left him, didn't I, Joe? I said I'm going to leave you because you ain't nothing. But he thought I was going to stay with him and cook for him and lay in bed with him. I said I'm going to leave you, baby, because you ain't nothing."

She saved her money while he "stuck his in a machine." She made a payment on a house as the couple was getting kicked out of his. She bought the house when he wasn't around, then came back to get her stuff.

"He said, 'Well, I'll be damned. Where you get money from to get a house?'" And she told him. She also told him he wasn't coming with her. He left her in rags in a rag place, she says, so she left him in rags. She took her refrigerator and her deep freezer. She left him the stove only because she had one to cook on already in the new place, and his had ants in it.

"And he thought I was going to take him back."

BUT ABOUT A YEAR LATER the man had a heart attack, a bad one. Heart failure. Geraldine took him back to take care of him. Her kids, now adults, brought him nice clothes. She bed-nursed him for fifteen days, "taking the water from him." The doctor had told him not to smoke or drink anymore. But it got to where she'd come home and the house would smell of smoke and there'd be liquor bottles in the back room. She kicked him out again and threw the clothes and his liquor bottles after him. Three years later, he turned up on her back door step, driving a white Cadillac, looking for money.

"I said, no, go on and die. And he went and died."

She turned out for his funeral in a black hat pulled down low across her eyes so nobody could see her laugh. She stood across the road watching as they "put him in the dirt. And his brothers and sisters standing there looking [at her]. I said, 'Damn you, you're gone.'"

He haunted her for two or three months after he died, Geraldine says. "He came back beside me, naked and burned up." She went to a psychiatrist, she said. The woman told her to get a piece of paper and write on it everything she could think about, how much he'd done to her and how mean he was, how he treated her and was going to leave her alone, carry it to the graveyard. That seemed to do it. But for two years a snake in her garden would show up behind her. The kids told her it was her husband. One day it followed her in the house, and she killed it.

"That man was such a mess. That man drove me crazy. I was so happy he burned," she said."

That's how it was.

———

SO JOE MOVED into the old trailer on the Moody place. He drank from the hose. He got his meals on that chest-high freezer in a utility room on the back porch, sitting on a stool. To an outsider it would have looked for all the world like chattel. It didn't look that way to Joe.

"At that time a lot of black folks ate out the back door, out under the trees. They fed them out the back door. The Moody family never fed me outdoors."

Copeland Moody paid Joe. He took him into town and bought him clothes at Kornblut's Department Store. He drove Joe each Sunday to Joe's own church, Spring Grove Baptist, down on the Mullins Highway a few miles farther than Moody's own, until the day Joe showed up driving a 1962 Ford Galaxy of his own. Moody pushed Joe to go to school—"pushed it and pushed it and pushed it," Jimmy says. "He loved Joe, I know that. He treated Joe just like he did me. He wanted Joe to be better, that's what Daddy wanted. Because Joe wanted to." Joe would sit up at night asking Copeland questions, about everything, until Copeland sighed, "Dang, boy, get up here and go to bed. Got to get out to work in the morning."

———

JIMMY LIVES about an hour away now, across the North Carolina line, and it's something to see the light in the two men's eyes when they grab hands.

Jimmy will smile at Joe's middle-age spread and tell him he's looking "a little Bunkish." It's a reference to an old man, Uncle Bunk, whom both of them knew and whom Joe slightly resembles. Uncle Bunk carried some heft to him. He had a '53 Chevrolet that he'd drive leaning on the door, so the car leaned too, and its shock absorbers would shimmy when he sat down.

The two will talk a while with a visitor, say goodbye, walk out to their cars, then sit on the tailgate of Jimmy's truck and talk some more. They are close enough that when Joe needed to speak with him one time, Jimmy got up in the dark and drove about an hour to meet him at a fast food place at the state line. At 7 A.M. When Jimmy and Joe talk, it's about family or it's about machines. They've got some tales, and both laugh when Jimmy tells how Joe ended up with a cultivator on top of him. A field cultivator is a piece of farm equipment that chews up the soil like a tiller, or a rake, to aerate it. Usually hooked to the

Jimmy Moody and Joe Williams. Courtesy of Cathy Petersen.

back of a tractor, it looks like a swath of fangs hanging like teeth of a denture. Well, the tractor got up on a bank and went over. Joe saw it coming quick enough to dodge but not quick enough to make it. He broke his leg, cut up the calf and hamstring, and cut his head. He was only twelve or thirteen years old. You don't think of farming as a contact sport, but there it is.

———

IF JOE HAS A LIMIT to his love for machines, it's two wheels. That, too, is a story he and Jimmy laugh about but Joe takes to heart. Jimmy took the younger Joe for a ride on a dirt bike one time, in 1972. They hit a bad spot, and Joe was thrown. "That broke me," Joe says. "I never, never got back on one." He's told both his kids he had better never catch them on a motorbike, either. Little Joe told him, "But I'm grown, Daddy." Joe told him, "I don't care. I'd better never catch you on a motorbike."

———

JOE HADN'T BEEN LIVING with the Moodys a year the day he and Jimmy were working on a water pump over at Jimmy's blockhouse. The metal was edged, and it didn't take long for Joe to nick a finger. Jimmy got in there and nicked a finger too. They looked at each other's fingers and laughed. Then they forged a children's bond.

"I just told him we were going to be blood brothers," Jimmy said. And he pressed his bloody finger onto Joe's. Just about anybody who grew up at that time has a story like that. What reverberates about this one is that these two men, in their fifties, each will tell it to you. They are blood brothers still.

Chapter 5

Cockleburs

LATTA SITS in the "Corridor of Shame," a stretch of poor, rural, and mostly black Midlands and Pee Dee communities along the I-95 corridor that covers forty school districts.

The districts' schools were the focus of a lawsuit against the state of South Carolina. They got the "shame" tag and national notoriety in a documentary on the conditions students had to go to school in. It's tough for anybody who grew up in a school with, say, clean toilets to appreciate how ratty some of these buildings were—sewage, scummy sinks, plywood desktops, and falling-apart books. The notoriety is enough of a stigma that Democratic candidates in the hotly contested 2008 primaries used the district to make photo-op points about the changes they would bring, and Barack Obama recognized a student from the district in his first State of the Union address, gesturing to the awestruck girl sitting in the Senate balcony with Michelle, his wife. It probably says more than you need to know about the Corridor that the defining civil rights moment of the 1950s, the Supreme Court ruling in *Brown vs. Board of Education,* stemmed from a lawsuit filed in Clarendon County, less than fifty miles down the road from Latta. A half-century went by between the Supreme Court ruling and the ensuing lawsuit against the state of South Carolina.

A number of Dillon County schools were included in the later lawsuit. None of them were in Latta. This is a town that takes a vocal pride in its schools. Joe lives on the line between Dillon and Marion Counties, and he made sure his children went to school in Latta, where he went to school. It's not by chance that coworkers at his mill tagged him with the nickname "Latta." That sense of cocoon, standing on its own, is almost visceral in this place. It's mellow. When the railroad gates drop at the tracks on Main Street, the alarm bell doesn't clang; it jingles.

Two years after Joe moved in with the Moodys, the town's schools integrated.

———

JOE'S OLDER SISTER, Earlene McKay, looks a lot like him and is a lot like him. At fifty-six years old, she's working three jobs. She's shy at first with a stranger. She listens intently and thinks before she speaks. She has a smile that's sweet and mischievous at the same time.

Going to a white school for the first time, she said, was "a little strange. You didn't know what to expect. You know, until integration, black people stayed on their side of town and white people stayed on this side of town."

But it turned out to be not anything, just going to school. There were some fights, sure, there was some mouthing off, but that wasn't any different from what happened in any other school year. Some people were troublemakers, but they were troublemakers anyway. In both races, Joe says. For most of the kids, sure, things were different. But school was just school. Put in the time. Besides, black or white, everybody knew most everybody else or knew somebody in their family.

"I'll tell you about Latta, this little town, this little community here. They'll argue against one another, they will do it. But they see one on the side of the road, white or black, they will stop and try to help him. This community here is like that," Joe says.

One of the ironic twists to the town's relatively sedate integration is that there weren't just two sets of schools in Latta.

"We had three schools," Geraldine says bluntly, "the black. The 'Croatan.' And the white." Whites kept to their side of town; black kept to their side of town.

"And the Indians, they stayed in the middle," Earlene said.

———

THE NAME "CROATAN" is a slur used regionally to describe people with native blood. It's considered vulgar, and the word can be as offensive as "nigger" to people with that blood. Croatans were members of one of the original Carolinas coastal tribes, a host of vaguely related and sporadically feuding peoples considered to have been largely Algonquin and Sioux. Croatans are thought to have lived primarily in the area of the Outer Banks in North Carolina. They were the tribe whose land was settled by the Lost Colony, that almost mythical early North Carolina community that "disappeared." Croatans, like the Lost Colony settlers and any number of coastal peoples, supposedly were wiped out by disease and the distempers of their new and old neighbors. But, as in any good myth, there's a haunt to the tale. Among the Lumbee tribe, which today can be found in the land between the Banks and the Pee Dee, there were early and inexplicable reports of blond hair. Word was the Lumbee blood included remnants of both the colonists and the Croatan. People—captive or not—moved from tribe to tribe in those days, and blood readily mixed. So, "Croatan" is one of those tags that can mean a few things, not all of them nice.

It's a dirty little secret of the region, smothered in all the ugliness of slave-free, black-white relations, that native peoples were looked down on by almost everyone else. A lot of their heritage has been lost simply because generations of descendants didn't talk about it, trying their best to "pass" unnoticed. When schools integrated, people with native blood felt the alienation harder than blacks. People just wouldn't talk to them, wouldn't sit near them in the lunchroom. Joe had friends who were native and didn't go for any of that stuff in school. When he showed up for school.

"Joe had not gone to school, what I would call going to school, up to that point," Jimmy Moody says about the move to the trailer. "Joe and I liked recess a whole lot."

Spring and fall, Joe was in the field. Any crop-tending excuse at all would keep him from opening bell. It was a love of the land, sure—and a pretty visceral lack of affection for the classroom.

"Every day it was like it was never going to end," Joe says about school. Copeland set out to change that, and when Copeland spoke, "that was it."

———

ISAIAH COLLINGTON wraps a long smile around his thin face. He wears big moon glasses. He was Joe's elementary school principal and one of his high school teachers, social studies. He is a distant cousin. They both live in Temperance Hill. He likes to say, "I never had money I could spend twice."

If you followed Joe's mom down a row, you learned how to sharecrop, Collington says. She was that good. "There has always been something about Joe that I loved," he goes on. "He's always had personality. He's always been honest. And he's always been willing to work. He may not have been the smartest kid on the block, academically. But I tell you one thing, he was the most trusted kid on the block. Joe worked at his lessons until he got them. He told the truth. If you caught him doing wrong, he fessed up."

———

IN THE SLAVEHOLDING DAYS the Latta area was not considered plantation country; it was planter country. Most farmers who held slaves kept from one to a dozen. And there's almost an absence of the ugliness in stories about slavery that permeates history in other places in the South. In 1937, a former slave, Hester Hunter Marion, talked about the old days on the John C. Bethea plantation as almost bucolic. The slaves got flour for Sunday eating. They had turnips, collards, and meat. They fished the farm pond and salted food away for the winter. "Never know nothing but big living," she said. And if she were sarcastic at all, it's a tough tell.

One historian notes that northern Marion County, the area that became Latta, didn't see much racial violence. There were no reports involving the Ku Klux Klan. A lot of the vehemence about slaves down in the Lowcountry and in Charleston had to do simply with the fact that there were a lot more work-hardened slaves than there were free whites. When rumors of an insurrection spread, like the Vesey uprising, in 1822, they spread terror.

In census after census around Latta, the numbers of blacks and whites are about the same. The first postmaster in Latta, in the 1890s, was Bob R. Bethea. Bethea is one of the iconic family names in the Pee Dee, the name of some of its first settlers. "Buck Swamp" John Bethea was the first farmer to begin ginning cotton, in 1798, purportedly with that cotton press standing outside town today, pulled by oxen or mules. Bethea is one of those names that was shared by both the families of former slaveholders and their former slaves. The 1890s were the Jim Crow era, the beginnings of codified segregation. Bob Bethea was black. He ran the post office out of his Main Street store. You can still find it. Latta, in fact, has one of those ubiquitous little town "historic districts," and if you take the sign seriously enough to go look, you will end up at a triangular patch of land across the street from the museum, a former dentist's office, and its rail car. The weather-beaten wood board old one-room building out front is Bethea's store. Inside are samples of the goods—a wooden washing machine, a scythe on the wall. The building is about the size of a modern living room. Tucked in the back corner, cordoned off by white-paint latticework, is the old post office, no bigger than a walk-in closet. The sign out front tells you that general stores of the time were the rural community meet-up spots. President Grover Cleveland appointed Bethea postmaster in 1890, "quite an honor for an African-American in an era of growing Jim Crow legislation."

Bethea served as postmaster for only three years.

———

DESPITE THAT "FEEL GOOD" sense of racial equanimity, bias threads right through the social weave of the place, the way it does through a lot of the South. People know you by your people, and your people are your place. An older, well-heeled white acquaintance of Joe's reassures a visitor that he's a very fine boy, doesn't think twice about asking Joe to find her help for her garden, but, she insists, no Mexicans.

Joe is consciously courteous to her. This is how things are. And it's how they were when the Pee Dee integrated. John Kirby and his wife, Vicki, were "the token white teachers" in one school when integration came to Mullins, just down the road from Latta, in 1972. Today the former history teacher is the superintendent of the Latta schools. He is a composed man with a kind look in his eye steeled over time and a grayed mustache and goatee. He has a habit of dipping his head toward you slightly as he makes a point and peering intently. He speaks with a slight chop of the words and has a wry edge of a smile as he listens. Like a good history teacher, he tends to think of things in a broader context. Kirby thinks of Joe as one of those characters that used to be found in every small town, it seems, people whose ways are eccentric enough to stand out and be recalled with fondness.

"Old school, Bohemian, eclectic, fly-the-seat. He's not just a character in his own community but across communities. It's a lost kind of character, a fading kind of culture," Kirby says. "He is one of the proudest men I know, and that exudes to his family."

The superintendent's office desk is lined with photos of grandchildren that face the visitors. A Mullins native, he decorates the office with tabletop replicas of buildings that are mementos of his youth—the period-piece Kirby Drug's building advertising air conditioning inside, an old schoolhouse, a rural country store like the one he used to haunt as a kid, and a tobacco packing house. In Pee Dee farm country, the story behind that doesn't need to be told.

Integration in Latta wasn't all that nice, Kirby says. There were fights. In the Pee Dee region, as in the rest of South Carolina, the era was the beginning of rural "academies," private schools started by well-to-do white families. All of them, Kirby says pointedly, were named after Confederate generals. As for integration, "I just think it was tolerated. It didn't create controversy," he says. The high schools in Latta and Mullins each burned down sometime during the 1970s, he adds. "You'll probably find coincidence there, but the older I get the harder it is to believe in coincidence."

The mood among whites at the time was that blacks were getting the better of the deal, Kirby says. And, you know, given the relative infrastructures of the two sets of schools, that would be easy to believe. But then Kirby says something a little startling. "I think the black community lost a lot more than the white community." The reason is pretty simple. That community looked to the halls of their schools—modest as they were—as social hubs, as much and maybe more than the smaller churches. Weddings were held at the schools, funerals, festivals, fairs.

"All of a sudden they lost all that," Kirby says. The halls became, for lack of any better way to say it, white. The community had to look for new rallying points. Churches didn't have the space. There were few buildings that did, fewer if any in the black communities. None held the proud legacy of the school.

"Integration," Kirby says pointedly, "was not the salvation of the black community that a lot of people thought it would be." The story he tells about it all, not so unexpectedly, has to do with mascots. With a decades-rich legacy of athletics, particularly football, Latta was the home of the Red Raiders. It was a point of heritage in the community, a lot more personal to residents than someone who did not grow up in a small rural place would realize. When talk came to sports, particularly football, graduates would tell you, "I'm a Red Raider."

When Mullins integrated, school officials directed that both schools keep their individual mascots and school colors, except that the former black high school became the junior high. When Latta integrated, they decided to do it differently, in deferential '60s style. The senior class was assigned to make new traditions. The red and blue Red Raiders became the green and lime-green Vikings, the name picked after the popular NFL team of the time, which had no particular connection to the town. The black Latimer High School's blue-and-gold Hornets simply disappeared. So, while on the surface at the new school it might have seemed that things were going smoothly, the reality was barbed. There were black and white homecoming queens, black and white proms. It was "separate but equal" segregation without the separation. Antagonism wasn't far beneath the surface. When Kirby took over as principal in the 1980s, he had to deal with a lawsuit over the issue of wearing Confederate-flag clothing.

"Was anybody fussing about that? No. Was it right? No," Kirby says. "It didn't bring the community together. It didn't do anything about hardened bad feelings. It was festering in everybody underneath, a little bit of turmoil."

That was the school that Joe—living with a white family—stepped into. Joe's situation could have been an example of what it could be, Kirby said. Instead, "He was the bane of everyone's existence. He was 'Uh oh. It could work.' He had people coming at him from all angles. He could have been just an ordinary, mean SOB. It would have been so easy for him to give up, get by, and just be an asterisk in history. Joe's not an asterisk. He is history."

––––––––

Well, I guess they done all right. I didn't ever mess around with them much. Like Irene saying she was his mother, she was saying . . . I ain't never got over it. I just went on.

Geraldine Williams

Joe's life with the Moodys was an eye-opener to his friends. George Legette used to make his way on Sundays down the Moodys' rich-people dirt drive to play with Joe. You ended up playing with the Moodys.

"They treated him like he was one of them, you know, like a brother or something like that. They joked with him, played with him, wrassled with him."

Joe became part of the family. Jimmy remembers Joe coming over to his house one time, and his one-year-old daughter, Amanda, began rubbing his hair. Joe takes up the story. "She took her hand and rubbed in my hair, she did. And she told her grandma, 'It feels like cockleburs,'" Joe says. "And oh, I started a-hollering." Amanda, Joe tells you, was his little princess. By then, Joe was Copeland Moody's hands and feet. He worked with Copeland if he wasn't working with Jimmy, and Copeland worked them both to the bone.

"I think he looked to us to stand in his stead," Jimmy says. "He had the mind to do it, but he didn't have the body that would go."

When Joe drives by the closed-up old Moody Agri Co. warehouse, he will point out where he put a few dents in the bay door, backing up the spreader truck to load and go to work. Charles Lane, the lifelong friend Joe met through the Moodys, remembers coming by the warehouse and finding Joe loading up spreader trucks with a shovel because the machine was torn up.

"If I was him I'd have gone back home," Lane laughs.

––––––––

J. G. Bryant is big, slow-talking country. He comes from one of the best-regarded tobacco farming families in the region. He started working mules when he was five years old. He sits in a chair with his legs tucked almost as if he were crouched. Joe looks up to him, thinks of him as the farmer who taught him most of what he knows.

"Joe would drive [Moody's] spreader truck, help around there with the fertilizer. I would find fertilizer for him. And I'd say, we'll catch up sometime. I don't know really what he did for Mr. Moody, but he helped him a lot 'cause he was kind of crippled. He had a hard time. He weren't a lazy man. He kept trying to go, to do things. And Joe stayed with him and helped him."

———

I wasn't crying or disappointed. You know, I figured it was something he wanted to and I didn't hold it against him. I didn't think it was a bad thing. They seemed to be, you know, all right people. We didn't know nothing bad about them. And they weren't really bad people. And the old man was just as good as he could be, Mr. Copeland. I liked him better than I did his wife. I didn't like it, no I didn't. I can say that after he got grown. But they didn't hurt Joe.

Earlene McKay

JOE MIGHT HAVE WON over Copeland pretty quickly, but Irene Moody was different. She grew up with a father who became debilitatingly arthritic in his twenties and died in his fifties. She married a man who grew debilitatingly arthritic in his twenties and died in his fifties. Her lot in life was not an easy one, as they say. Dour faced, with a yearning in her eye, she wanted things her way and she wanted them now. She could cook up a storm. When the house got a heating system and Copeland, struggling with arthritis, was slow to get rid of the fireplace she didn't like in the family room, Irene grabbed a sledge and tore apart the bricks herself. Joe remembers having to take down the chimney.

Irene Moody was a handful.

"Momma could aggravate you," Jimmy says. "She could stay on your case. Daddy told you and you could take it to the bank. Momma would tell you over and over and when she told you enough, she'd say, 'I'm going to tell your daddy.' Daddy would get to where he was in extreme pain and still be going. Daddy went until he couldn't go. She wanted a lot of things and Daddy couldn't provide."

A telling story about the Moodys is that after Joe had been with the family two years Copeland decided to buy him a bigger trailer, no doubt at the pestering of Irene, who came along with the two of them to make sure it was done right. She found a trailer she liked the color of. The price tag was $3,500. Copeland shooed her off.

Irene and Copeland Moody. Courtesy of Joe Williams.

"Eighteen hundred dollars is more my color," Joe mimics Copeland. "Back up, back up. That boy he doesn't like that one. That one right there. Sitting right there." Jimmy laughs, remembering the story. "Daddy wanted it to his liking, which was his pocketbook's liking." They came home with a ten-foot by thirty-five-foot trailer. It was still one room, but a long, skinny room rather than the fat closet Joe was living in. It had a kitchen.

Even more telling might be Irene's apparent motivation. Virginia Merchant is Copeland's only sister, his youngest and only living sibling. At eighty-two, she has one of those rumply, impishly sweet faces you associate with a leprechaun and the kind eyes that remind you of Jimmy Moody, her nephew.

She was a companion to Irene and Copeland, joined them on long rides as a pastime. She remembers how they would stop at the C & S grocery in Dillon, buy bread and bologna, and make impromptu picnic lunches right there.

Joe became more a part of the family as Copeland became more crippled, eventually all but running the place, physically lifting Copeland and helping him get clothes on in the morning. Copeland treated him like one of his own, and "Aunt Ginnie" thought of him as family, as she does today. It riled her to see Joe eating in the utility room. And dinner at the Moodys became more and more awkward with Joe sitting back on that freezer while the rest of them were in the kitchen. Aunt Ginnie thought he belonged at the table, and she thinks Copeland did too. But there was nothing to be said. Irene wouldn't have stood for it.

"At the same time she appreciated Joe, she could give him living hell," Aunt Ginnie says. Her voice breaks a little when she talks about Joe.

"The things he did for Copeland. He was his hands, his feet. Can you see him putting, Joe, putting him in the bathtub, a big man, two hundred pounds, in the bathtub every day? Seeing he got in his car or truck right, that he had his farm operation carried out right? He was called on, Joe was on call for him twenty-four hours a day." That as much as anything might explain Irene's motivation for wanting the trailer.

Joe lived with the Moodys for eight years before he moved from the utility room to the kitchen bar to eat. By then he was in the house all the time anyhow to take care of Copeland. The next year, 1975, Copeland Moody died. Irene Moody went to talk to the trustee board of the Ebenezer Southern Methodist Church. In nearly two hundred years of existence the church had never had a person who was black attend services. Would it be all right, she asked, if Joe attended Copeland's funeral? If not, she would just have the service in the funeral home, she said.

It's a testament to the board as well as to Joe that there was little if any hesitation. Joe is part of the family, Irene Moody was told. It's a testament to Copeland Moody that Joe was one of three people from his community who did attend.

After Copeland's death, Joe moved to the family table. He was twenty-one years old.

Chapter 6

Washed in the Clouds

I heard that he was a friend to Abraham Lincoln, but they never did print that out. I heard the old people talking about it.

Geraldine Williams

THE LINCOLN STORY is a headshaker. It could well be another one of those tales from deeply held freedmen lore, accounts of Lincoln turning up in communities during the war. It's got that resonant real-time feel of a parable.

But Aunt Lou was specific about Scipio Williams being one of a group of men Lincoln met in the White House kitchen, and she was Scipio's daughter.

If the story is true, it would to an extent rewrite Lincoln history—a tale about which there wouldn't seem to be a whole lot more to tell. Thousands of books have been written about the Great Emancipator. Amazon.com alone lists more than fourteen thousand entries on a search for books about him. His papers are on file and available online at the Library of Congress. You can find a day-by-day record of what he did, literally a journal, online at lincolnlog.org, and most of the recent literature is little more than a reanalysis of those records. And that was before the election of Barack Obama, which led to an upswell of interest in Lincoln as another wave hits the shore. You would think that every rock had been turned over by both admirers and contemptuous detractors who blame Lincoln for what they consider a dictatorial, bloody, devastating invasion.

For sure, the meeting was unlikely. I couldn't find a mention of Scipio, White House kitchen meetings, or a meeting with Carolinas freedmen in the Library of Congress papers or in the log.

Roger Norton, creator of the online Abraham Lincoln Research Site, was among four Lincoln researchers I contacted to see if they had come across anything like the meeting in their records search. He hadn't. But, interestingly enough, considered in terms of the widespread folklore of Lincoln visits to freedmen, Norton noted that the question had not come up before—among more than fifty thousand inquiries he gotten about Lincoln over the course of his career. This isn't your usual freedmen lore.

That's what makes Aunt Lou's story so compelling.

———

LOU'S RECOLLECTION of a "kitchen" meeting hints at some sort of clandestine thing, even though kitchens were the household common ground between the races back then. If the meeting was a kind of backdoor intelligence gathering, it surely would have been surreptitious. Solicitation of that sort wasn't going to make its way into the record, not there, not then. If Lincoln were known to be turning to freedmen for intelligence, the politics of the day would have done him in well before Booth's bullet.

But the record is plain that he did meet with blacks, socially as well as formally, and the frequency of documented encounters is enough to suggest there were more. In *The Fiery Trial*, the historian Eric Foner notes that Lincoln met with five ministers from North Carolina seeking the right to vote, with a number of groups of black clergymen, and with two emissaries from the freedmen community in New Orleans, among others.

Foner's information on the meetings came from the *Anglo-African Weekly*, a New York–based publication that was one of the emerging black periodicals of the time. The North Carolina ministers' meeting is reported in the May 14, 1864, edition. The item, retrieved courtesy of the Houghton Library at Harvard University, is curious for a few reasons. Unlike other reports in the edition, it carries no date of its own. Because it's reported as news, the meeting would appear to have occurred sometime not long before the printing, in the spring of 1864. That would be about the time or shortly before the bloody Battle of the Wilderness took place around Fredericksburg, Virginia. That the meeting took place at all suggests that, even in the midst of the fighting, there was travel back and forth between the Carolinas and D.C., enough of it that the writer makes no mention of how the ministers got there.

"A delegation, consisting of the gentlemen whose names are attached to the petition, called on the President, and presented it," the item reads. "Their interview was a pleasant one, and they received from Mr. Lincoln assurances of his sympathy and earnest cooperation."

The petition invokes the "all men are created equal" line from the Declaration of Independence and calls on Lincoln to finish the noble work he had started (with the emancipation of Southern slaves). The item is headlined "FREEMEN OF NORTH CAROLINA STRIKING FOR THEIR RIGHTS."

———

SCIPIO WILLIAMS was born and raised and lived his life in the country around today's Latta, as near as anyone can say so far. His father was born in Virginia and sold to a slaveholder in South Carolina. Queen Gordon, who has done the most extensive family genealogical research, hasn't been able to determine whether Scipio had brothers or sisters—although, given the times and his father's slavery, he very likely did. Then as now, the name Williams was so common among both blacks and whites and the records are so piecemeal that there isn't any point to making much of the coincidence that one of the five gentlemen who signed the freedmen petition was Jarvis M. Williams.

———

ON TOP OF ALL THAT is Lincoln's notorious "firster," a formal public meeting with a group of Washington-area ministers that gets touted as unprecedented and that deriders as well as apologists seize on to prove their point about how racist or not Lincoln was.

In 1862, earlier in the war, the president and Congress set aside $600,000 and looked into resettling or "colonizing" blacks—simply removing them from the United States, shifting the history of slavery into reverse. African countries were looked at first, then Central and South American countries. Resettlement as an idea had knocked around politically for years by the time of the war and would continue to be knocked around for at least a half-century more. By Lincoln's administration, some blacks as well as whites had been promoting the idea for more than a generation without much success. Even today, African roots run deep for any number of families who trace their heritage to slavery. The Gullah traditionalists in the South Carolina lowcountry cling tightly to their West African ways, and those who can manage it make that now classic *Roots* trip back across the ocean to find their folk. In the lowcountry near Saint Helena, there's the Kingdom of Oyotunji, a handful of families inspired by a "king" of shaky reputation. They live in a close-to-the-dirt commune with the colorful robes and spirited customs of an African village.

Colonization was the "moderate" view of the time, as Foner documented. It was Lincoln's public stance on the matter, as much as one could really divine his public stance. Lincoln was politically shrewd enough to temper what he suggested to suit his listener. Caller after caller came away from meeting with Lincoln convinced the president was on his or her side, Foner notes. For every documented instance of Lincoln taking the colonization stance, there seems to be another where he suggests that his support of the idea is little more than a tactic. Lincoln also floated options such as gradual emancipation, usually at least implying gradual resettlement, to appease the jumpy "border" states that might go Confederate.

Then, on August 14, the president summoned a delegation of five leading Washington-based ministers to tell them they had to go. He didn't talk; he lectured. He had a stenographer in the room, making it certain that the meeting would quickly get out to the press. What strikes me about that meeting: First, it pretty obviously wasn't a firster; second, how a group of ministers so initially hostile to the idea of resettling an entire population in another country so quickly came around to support it.

Lincoln's words and his tone don't leave much wriggle room for the whole "Great Emancipator, Father of the Race" thing:

> You and we are different races. We have between us a broader difference than exists between almost any other two races. Whether it is right or wrong I need not discuss, but this physical difference is a great disadvantage to us both, as I think your race suffers very greatly, many of them, by living among us, while ours suffers from your presence. . . . We look to our condition, owing to the existence of the two races on this continent. I need not recount to you the effects upon white men growing out of the institution of slavery. I believe in its general evil effects on the white race. . . . But for your race among us there could not be war, although many men engaged on either side do not care for you one way or the other. Nevertheless, I repeat, without the institution of slavery, and the colored race as a basis, the war would not have an existence. . . . It is better for us both, therefore, to be separated.

There's a little voice in my head telling me they didn't come there to hear that. What gnaws at me about this meeting is the staged feel to it. The tone is almost oratorical compared to how Lincoln talks to Frederick Douglass—who was fiercely opposed to resettlement—or Sojourner Truth in anecdotes I will describe shortly. It has that set piece, Gettysburg Address feel to it. The remarks don't have the ring of a real sell to a group of hostile ministers. They sound more like the sort of thing you might say to them in front of a mob of angry whites.

The tone of this well-publicized "first" meeting suggests it was a presidential performance, that something else was really taking place. This was Washington, after all. What if it was all a show, the equivalent of today's photo op, a say-all-the-right-things session that masked the real discussion? Looked at realistically, a few million people scattered throughout the country weren't going to be easily moved anywhere, much less for $600,000, even at 1860s prices. The cost alone would be prohibitive. Yet, within four days, the Reverend Edwin Thomas, the delegation chairman, wrote Lincoln to say that he was now open to considering the idea and asked Lincoln's authorization to travel among his friends and coworkers to convince them. Within a month, the government contracted with Ambrose Thompson to develop the Chiriqui colony in Brazil—but only if he could get the local authorities there to agree to it. Thompson had to operate on the promise of $50,000 once he got the effort started. A small colonization effort did eventually take place and fails miserably.

Meanwhile, Lincoln got back to work on the Emancipation Proclamation.

———

ALL THIS TOOK PLACE during a critical phase of the war, the year of the first great Union offensives, mass bloodshed, and small-scale victories. Lincoln needed to reassure a very antsy white population and maybe even himself, to give him a little room to maneuver and them a little time to get used to the idea that from now on things were going to be Different. On the face of it, Thomas's rapid turnaround on the colonization question suggests there had been some behind-the-curtain discussion. And the ministers had reason to play along.

Some forty thousand "contraband" and freed men, women, and children converged on a not-so-welcoming Washington during the war. Contraband camps were thrown together in squalor, and they were overrun with tents. Race relations around the capital weren't any better than they are today. Freedmen suddenly seemed to be everywhere, and they were the very visible face of a future that made a lot of whites very uneasy. Roving mobs beat up on them. But when Lincoln and Mrs. Lincoln made their way from the White House to their cottage by the Soldiers Home, they would stop by the camp on Seventh Street to hear freedmen sing spirituals and . . . mmmhmm . . . make no effort to ask where people came from and how it was back home, where a few hundred thousand troops were now blasting away at one another. The stops weren't spontaneous; the singers knew to dress up.

This is the man who walked through the streets of newly taken Richmond in 1865 swarmed by people of color, laughed, and shook hands as he was pressed by folks who just wanted to touch him, while his bodyguards pulled their bayonets, worried over his safety. Then he met with freedmen there.

———

ONE INTRIGUING little footnote to Civil War history is the recent revelation that the Union used blacks in servant roles as spies and did it a lot more pervasively than anyone admitted at the time. The official records of the practice are almost nonexistent—destroyed by spymasters for a number of reasons, chiefly the safety of the spies involved—and a lot of what is known about it comes from African American oral histories. No less a Confederate than General Robert E. Lee in 1863 called black spies the chief source of information for the enemy.

————

LINCOLN HAD A RELATIVELY INTIMATE, teasing relationship with Elizabeth Keckley, his wife's dressmaker. Keckley is the source that provides maybe the best voice-of-the-times perspective on Lincoln's take on colonization: "Many colored people were in Washington and large numbers had desired to attend the [re-election] levee, but orders were issued not to admit them," she writes as a prelude to telling how Lincoln requested that the esteemed black orator Frederick Douglass be brought in and introduced to him at the gala. Lincoln "pressed his hand warmly, saying: 'Mr. Douglass, I am glad to meet you. I have long admired your course, and I value your opinions highly.'"

Typically of Lincoln, the comment is at the same time decorously social, politically shrewd in what it says and what it doesn't say to both detractors and admirers, and maybe even a little personally revealing, at least to Douglass, who opposed resettlement. It's interesting that biographers of Sojourner Truth credit Keckley with arranging for the abolitionist to meet Lincoln. And that meeting wasn't just a handshake. In a simple, honest reply to some over-the-top praise from Truth, Lincoln told her he wouldn't have freed the slaves if he had not been compelled to. And, in fact, he freed slaves only in the states that were in rebellion and told advisors it was a war strategy.

In other words, Lincoln was a man holding in each hand the fuses people kept lighting on a big powder keg in a magazine that already was going up in flames. He needed to work both ends against the middle.

————

SCATTERED IN among the Lincoln papers are earnest appeals by Southern freedmen seeking land or seeking reassurance they could keep the plots they worked. They are from South Carolina. And Lincoln took actions to set aside plots of land for freed slaves. It was no idle concern. The war was fought over property, including human property, as much as anything. The wealth in the South that wasn't counted in bodies was counted in acres, and as the wilting cotton economy and then the war shriveled up that wealth, Southerners white and black fought to hang onto their tatters.

Land was life for freedmen. Before the war they tended to be skilled crafts-people who could earn their papers. But they made obeisances to and depended on whites for income in a relationship that wasn't far removed from indentured servitude. Land gave them their own, provided food and essentials. They needed every clod of it. Outside Charleston, only one in every hundred African Americans was freed before the war, and attitudes toward them became uglier and uglier as they earned wealth and found their voice in the prewar years. Legislative moves were made to re-enslave the population or at least get them out of the state.

————

THE FAMILY LORE of Scipio doesn't account for how he acquired his land. The lore says Scipio was a freedman before the war. In the 104th-birthday interview, Aunt Lou recalled that both her parents were slaves freed after the war. Queen Gordon, a family genealogy researcher, doubts that. Scipio was born, serendipitously enough, on Christmas Day in 1836. That makes him young to be freed before the war, much less to have held land. He married a much younger Laura Crawford in 1860, when she was twelve or thirteen and more than ten years his junior. Because of the age difference, Queen suspects he was freed by then or at least had the wherewithal to make such a match.

It might be that both are true. In 1841, when Scipio was a small child, the state banned the freeing of slaves. It's hard to say how much real difference that made in the rural country of Marion County. Relations between blacks and whites then were as nuanced as the more-than-occasional family resemblance between master and "property" and as layered as the laws governing how much white blood you had to have before anybody was going to think of you as white. Before 1800, freeing slaves was an occasional custom, a kind of reward for good service by masters who maybe had more than a twinge of guilt. The practice was frowned on more and more as slave trading was done away with and freedmen established themselves. Not that everybody quit freeing their slaves. Some just handled it more subtly. The state ban was directed partly at stopping a practice of virtually freeing slaves by deeding them to friends who acted as guardians rather than owners, as Walter Edgar points out in *South Carolina: A History*. The 1880 census, when Scipio was forty-three years old and almost certainly a landholder, lists him as a "farm laborer." In a later census, his land holdings are understated. In those days, as Queen notes, if white people came around with sheets of paper and started asking you questions, it wasn't necessarily in your best interests to tell them the whole truth.

"Only way I can see, because back in those days it was tough for a black man, Scipio Williams had some kind of connection," Joe says. "If he could get 390 acres of land back in them days, he had somebody saying, 'Y'all don't touch him. You'd better not mess with him.'"

There's a world of truth in that. An 1822 South Carolina law required freedmen to have a white guardian. Not so coincidentally, maybe, Scipio was raised by a white man who owned a sizeable tract of land. Scipio had a very marketable skill as a carpenter. He would make a name for himself woodworking coffins. He made the furniture in his home, made his children's shoes.

―――――

IN BLACK MASTERS: *A Free Family of Color in the Old South,* the authors focus on William Ellison's skill at making cotton gins as the key not only to his wealth but to his freedom—freedom he bought from his white owner. Ellison was older than Williams; he freed himself in the more tolerant times before the 1822 law requiring a guardian. He lived near Sumter, not too far from today's Latta. Considered the wealthiest freedman of his time, he owned nearly nine hundred acres at one point.

―――――

THE YEARS JUST BEFORE THE WAR, when Scipio was raised, were tough times for freedmen trying even to keep their freedom. Those bills to re-enslave them kept cropping up in the legislature. None passed, but at least one came very close to passing. If a freed person left the state he or she couldn't come back except by petitioning the legislature—and you can imagine how that would go. The mood was uncomfortable enough that freedmen who could moved north or to Canada. The Pinckney family of Ten Mile near Awendaw tells the story about how their property was founded by a freedman ancestor who left Charleston before the war to live on remote Capers Island, which was at that time an isolated barrier island across Compahee Sound, out of the way of the channels or any real attention. Not until after a hurricane in the early 1870s did he pick up the ruins of his house and float them piece by piece back across the sound to found Pinckney Estates.

―――――

THE HALF-CENTURY BEFORE the Civil War was a boom period for the Pee Dee. Cotton stuck itself onto the region big time. The plantings doubled the income of growers and tripled the value of land, Eldred E. Prince notes in *Long Green: The Rise and Fall of Tobacco in South Carolina.*

And in boom times, people are more magnanimous. In South Carolina in 1860, free men—black and white—were among the wealthiest people in the nation. Even in backcountry Marion County, the per capita income was more than $26,000 per year (in 1996 dollars), according to Edgar. Those dollars alone would have made South Carolina freedmen of interest to Washington.

———

CONVENTIONAL WISDOM would say there's no way Scipio could pull off a trek from the Pee Dee to the Potomac in the midst of a war being fought over a lot of the same ground. But plenty of others made it—in fact, relatively easily. Travel and communications evidently weren't as difficult as conventional histories suggest. The *Anglo-African Weekly* item about that North Carolina ministers' meeting with Lincoln notes that the petition the freedmen carried was the product of several meetings in different parts of the state. Most of the D.C.-area refugees came from nearby Virginia, but not everyone did. Freedmen camps were scattered through the South, causing no end of headaches for their Army tenders. In the middle of the war, two Quaker schoolteachers came down from Pennsylvania to set up the Penn School on Saint Helena Island in the South Carolina lowcountry and helped freedmen there petition Lincoln to keep their lands.

———

"Wow," said Emory Campbell when he heard the story of Scipio. Campbell is a revered community leader among the Gullah people on the South Carolina coast. He has spent his life researching and promoting their West African origins and the cultural history that literally built—shackled hand over shackled hand—the Lowcountry. He served as executive director of the Penn Center, the historical and cultural institution that emerged from the schoolhouse where those Quaker teachers taught. Campbell points out that freedmen on Saint Helena Island did set up a government during the war, although it was under the direction of Union commanders. It's possible the same thing was going on in other locations, he said.

Scipio Williams reputedly was a founding member of Andrews Chapel United Methodist Church in Latta, where Aunt Lou worshipped all her life and taught catechism until she became too feeble.

Joe recalls hearing that Scipio was a council member, a sort of assemblyman for freedmen in his region. It's not that big a reach. The Gullah communities of the lowcountry had a deep-rooted tradition of the "meeting tree," stemming from the long-lived African baobab, and African-American churches of the time amounted to quasi-social governments for their congregations.

OTHER HISTORIANS or archivists contacted for this story agreed there's no mention of anything like a kitchen meeting in the Lincoln repositories. Harlan Greene, of the Avery Research Center, the black history and cultural institution at the College of Charleston, speculated that the Williams family might have mixed memories, that Scipio might have met with a later president as an established landholder or possibly a militia leader. An 1869 enrollment of militia in Marion County lists a Scipio Williams; it is pretty sure that this was one of the freedmen militias said to have started forming only a few years earlier, after Lincoln was killed.

Ira Berlin, the University of Maryland historian who has studied slave and freedmen accounts more than maybe anyone else, said the Washington trip sounded unlikely for a number of reasons. The logistics would have made it "a very chancy adventure" during the war. It would have taken place more likely after the war—leaving a window of only a few weeks before Lincoln's death. Berlin said that if a freedman owned much property before the war, he might well have been a leader in the black community.

"I am careful not to discount the histories that flow through family lines," he said. "They prove true more often than not or at least have a kernel of truth."

SCIPIO "was a big ol' nice-looking, fine-lookin' man," Geraldine says. "Scipio was something."

He was something, all right. Scipio was a tailor as well as a carpenter and a farmer—a handy set of skills for a slave, much less a man in bondage looking for freedom or the father of a large country household of children.

He evidently made his life and his wealth through some of the worst times of the Pee Dee, postwar years of bitter prejudices, poverty, and near-starvation for some, when cotton was what you grew and the price fell and fell to ruin. His daughter, Lou, recalled the powerful 1886 earthquake. In 1893 a hurricane tore through the Pee Dee, ravaging crops and livestock—in the midst of a depression that Eldred Prince, in *Long Green*, describes as all but choking off business in the area, leaving cotton farmers unable to sell the crops, what was in essence an economic drought. That kicked cotton prices to the curb; the farmers couldn't get

Letters Testamentary of Scipio Williams, with two "X" signatures. Courtesy of Benton Henry Photography.

any more for the crop than the cost to grow it. The lenders, naturally, grabbed the land they held as equity, not that there was much they could do with it.

These were years when farmer after farmer in the Pee Dee gave up cotton for tobacco. By the early 1900s, when warehouses opened throughout the Pee Dee, tobacco would give the region its second boom. The crop was so profitable it brought the railroad, so profitable that as the line was run through Dillon, just north of Latta, on a straight bead to Savannah, Georgia, a spur line kicked southeast to the little town of Mullins, which had become a lucrative center for shipping tobacco.

Tobacco became the go-to crop and stayed that way to at least some extent into Joe's farming days. But there's no indication in Scipio's estate that he grew it. One of the biggest assets in the estate when he died was a corn crop still in the field.

By the time of Scipio's death, he and Laura had sixteen surviving children all told. He rang the children in from the fields with a handbell each day for morning prayer. He told them he washed his hands in the clouds.

The file of his Letters Testamentary is surprisingly thick for its time, even by the estimation of the Marion County archivist who retrieved it. The one human shred of Scipio dangling out from the brittle, yellowed papers is his signature. It's an "X." The scrawl rivets you on an 1898 bill of sale of 128 acres to Scipio. It's a backslash with a forward slash through it, the opposite of what you'd expect. The backslash bows back to its left. The forward slash is straight and emphatic, like the final flourish on a signature. It's thickest where it crosses the backslash, suggesting a "make no mistake" emotion. In a few checks written for farm supplies shortly before Scipio died, the "X" is more standard, maybe scrawled by the same hand that wrote his signature in full, suggesting maybe that he was pretty ill or maybe that someone else had control of the checkbook.

Unlike a will, the letters aren't an intact record. They're glimpses of Scipio's later years and a series of shake-your-head snatches of sniping among the children over the division of his estate.

Scipio died on July 22, 1903, leaving four children still at custodial ages, although the oldest was twenty and the others well into their teens. He also left "a large crop of corn" in the field, and that was no small thing. Corn was fetching some of the best prices it had in twenty years, and the corn harvested for the estate brought in $1,200. Among the documents are papers dealing with harvest and sale of this crop under probate. The children didn't end up with $800 each. They did end up with cash or items representing nearly $400 each—a sum worth tens of thousands in today's money. But they sold a large chunk of the land to do it and to satisfy debts, "so much thereof as may be necessary," according to a court summons. It's not clear how much land Scipio had, but the papers indicate at least 338 acres and maybe as many as 348 acres. In one odd paper filed in October, in the midst of settling the estate, Frank Williams appears to sign over 348 acres, "my entire interest in my father Scipio Williams' estate," to satisfy a $45 debt to a general store. That may be the origin of the "sold the land for syrup" story that the family remembers Aunt Lou telling. The store ended up with a $45 check from the estate.

Among a pile of interesting side notes in the papers is that 1898 bill of sale. Some 128 acres were sold to Scipio for $1,772.70 under an agreement on his part to pay $20 per month. Scipio had substantial debt when he died, in nineteenth-century terms. According to one accounting in the papers, the estate owed a final $364 payment on the $1,772 debt for the 128 acres and various $100-plus debts to the general store, supply store, and other provisioners, a total debt of more than $1,000. The estate in August paid $123.81 on a $723.81 bill to the Latta Supply Company for a variety of supplies from plow points to lard, salt, and candy. The remainder, you could suppose, was at least one of the outstanding bills settled by the sale of the land. The heirs prepared to auction as many as 338 acres in January 1904, including those 128 acres. A March 1904 accounting in the papers noted that 255 acres were sold, evidently all that was needed to pay the debt.

A number of the adult children took some of their estate shares in personal property, and the property they wanted suggests there was more land to farm, although in farm country there really weren't many other options besides share-cropping or tenant farming. Judging from the papers, Aunt Lou took a lion's share of the household goods, likely because she and the custodial children remained in the house: The load of the goods alone suggests a "stay put." She culled a good share of the food supplies and livestock, including twenty-five barrels of corn, four barrels of peas, a sow pig, ten turkeys and seven chickens.

Lou later told the family she helped raise her four youngest siblings. The papers suggest they may have continued to live with her and her sister Fanny, at least for the few years they remained minors. Lou shared with Fanny an oven, a range, two pots, four bowls, a mule, four lamps, two clocks, a wardrobe or closet, three wash stands, seventeen quilts, nine sheets, a safe and "crochery" (crockery, or tableware—which might have had some value if it came with the safe), eight beds, four bureaus, a carpet and a rug, two sofas, a "machine," six pictures, and an organ and stool. The way the family heard it, Lou also hung on to some small portion of the land.

The older children divided among themselves a big share of the farm tools, animals, and household items. According to the inventory for the childrens' shares and auction, Scipio's personal property included three mules and a mare, a new buggy and an old buggy, a surrey and a wagon, four plows, four cotton plows, and a set of carpenter's tools, $100 worth of cows, sixteen turkeys, more than a dozen chickens, and nearly a dozen pigs of one sort or another.

The furnishings from his home all told were more remarkable—thirty-five chairs, four bureaus, twenty-two wash pots, three wash tubs and stands, two sofas, an oven, and a range. All of the furniture presumably was made by Scipio.

———

THERE ARE INDICATIONS in the papers of a lot of tugging back and forth among the children over the estate. An August 1903 petition in the Court of Pro-bate deals with the unsuccessful efforts by five of the adult children to remove Edward, the oldest, as executor, whom they testified they didn't trust. It opens by stating that Scipio died "leaving considerable real and personal property," then lays into it: "at the first meeting of the heirs subsequent to the death of their father they unanimously agreed that Edward was the proper one to adminis-ter, but that subsequently some friction had come about among the heirs . . . it appears to the Court that the heirs of Scipio Williams have become divided into two factions, and that the differences are of recent origin." The court sides with Edward, but orders him to turn over a $3,000 bond, to ensure the "the faithful discharge of his duties."

Edward, as it turns out, ends up with more than twice as much as the other heirs, including nearly $455 "by commissions," apparently for acting as executor. A quirky little footnote to the whole record is that the probate judge handling the estate, P. B. Hamer, billed the estate $33 in September as an insurance agent, evidently for a policy payment.

———

THE BOTTOM LINE is that Scipio Williams left a sizeable estate, and the way the family remembers it is pretty close to what it was. Dig hard enough into any hard-to-crack myth and there's a little pearl of truth, or at least a bit of it. The story that Scipio met with Lincoln could be just one more piece of a proud folklore, a sort of parable. But Aunt Lou was specific. Her dad was one of a group of men who met with Lincoln in the kitchen.

"Let me tell you something about a Williams," Joe says. "They'll go through a lot, but if a Williams really wants to help something in life and they make their mind up, the only way you'll stop a Williams trying to get something is just let his breath out of his body."

Chapter 7

Tough Love

AT A GAS STATION, a man sees Joe pumping gas and comes on over:
"Hey, Joseph, how you doin'? I recognize you drivin' that big old Ford there, boy. I got you drivin' that big old nice Ford. I need a four-hitch, a four-hitch bush hog."

"A four-hitch bush hog?"

"You got one at the house?"

"Joe [James, called Joe], I don't know. I just hauled off my, a lot of junk."

"Holy..."

"I don't, Joe, for offhand, I sure don't. What kind of site you plan to put a sun up, you know what I'm talking about."

"Sue Bay."

"The one I had, Joe, is a fast hitch. And it wore completely out. It's in weeds up to the trees. I wouldn't need the headache, just to be honest with you."

"OK, I'll holler at you later.... Man tried to let me have a new one for $500. Said he paid $670 for it a couple of years. Said he'd let me have it for $500. That a pretty good deal?"

"Yeah, yeah, yeah. You got $500?"

"Said it would fit me pretty good. Wouldn't nobody else buy it."

"Yeah, that's a good deal. Would it fit you in Sue Bay, or do you have to have a fast hitch? It would? Yeah, yeah, yeah. That's a good deal."

"All right. I'll see you later."

"I'll see you later."

"Went to high school with him," Joe says.

―――――

JOE FLUNKED first grade. That was in a country school in Marion County. In March the next year, 1962, his mom moved out of her parents' house and took the children a little way down the road to Dillon County, where the schools were better. But he stayed out of school the rest of that year. He remembers her taking him, his twin sister, Judy, and Earlene out onto the porch of that tenant farmer shack on a hot day the next September to tell them they weren't going to go to school. She didn't have decent clothes to put on them.

"I'm not going to send my kids to school in rag clothes," she said. It kicked something in his mind, he said, even then. He told himself if he ever had kids, they were going to be able to dress to go to school.

He and his siblings grew up rough. Joe's childhood friend George Legette has known Joe so long they have that easy, joking-around rapport. Asked what Joe was like as a kid, George gets a serious face. "Mean as hell." Then he and Joe break up laughing. But there's something to it. Joe's brother Melvin had a reputation for throwing rocks. Kids in the neighborhood would be kept out of school to pick cotton. And when you picked cotton you got picked on by the other kids. That came with the territory. You've got to do what you have to do. Even as teens George and Joe drove the school bus in the morning, then got out of school to pick. "It was really the only industry we had," Legette said.

So by the time Joe moved in with the Moodys he was an ambivalent, if ambitious, student. He was out of school all the time. When he was there he joked and jived, George remembers, talked about tractors and how he was going to be one of the biggest farmers around. He heard the goads, for sure.

In one of those misstabs at tough-love mentoring that ends up haunting a kid's memory for life, a school administrator stopped Joe as he walked out of the cafeteria one day. He was in the eighth grade when he should have been in the tenth grade, still falling behind because of the hours he put in at the farm and with Copeland. He had been sitting at the table with white students. The administrator, apparently monitoring the lunch, motioned him over.

"He looked at me and said, 'Hey. C'm'here,'" Joe says, and his face gnarls as he recalls it. "And he said, 'You'll never be nothin'.' He told me. And I said, 'What are you sayin'? Why are you sayin' that about me?' And he said, 'You just won't never be nothin', son. I see you staying around school for a long time. I'll never see you turn out to be nothin'.' I said, 'Well, OK. You wait and see.'" He said, "Are you talkin' back to me, son? I'll burn your britches.' And I said, "Well, if I'm talkin' back, I'm talkin' back.'"

―――――

JOE HAD THIS RESTLESS, relentless drive. George remembers a backyard project they worked on, trying to rebuild a Ford Falcon for George, out in the yard in the cold and dark. The master cylinder was shot, it turned out. George's mom was calling him to come in, but Joe wouldn't let it go. George had had enough— "Aw, man, you need a new one." And Joe wouldn't hear it. "Come on, George. We can fix this one. We can fix this one."

Copeland pushed Joe to go to school. "He pushed it and pushed it and pushed it," Jimmy said. "Joe went to school after we moved him in. That was one thing Daddy was going to make sure he did." It might even have been part of the agreement with Geraldine. At thirteen, Joe got his first report card to be signed by "his white daddy," in the words of Virginia Merchant, Copeland's sister. Joe still has it.

Joe had been with the Moodys only two years when Copeland declared bankruptcy and sold the farmland around the house at auction. It was in the winter, before Christmas. Crippled and in pain, Copeland just couldn't do it anymore.

IT'S HARD FOR ANYBODY who didn't grow up in a rural small town to appreciate how religious the fervor is for high school sports, particularly football. It's Friday Night Lights, blood, kith and kin. The mark of a man is, did he play ball. Joe can reel off from the top of his head everyone from Latta who played pro ball or had a shot at it. He can tell you what team each one of the active players is with now. Every time he drives by the old high school he mentions Raymond Felton, who led the Carolina Tarheels to a national championship and now plays in the NBA. Joe's not a betting man, he'll tell you, but he'll put $20 on a Latta football game.

Any conversation between Joe and a high school acquaintance sooner or later drifts toward the glory days. Sitting with Clement Epps, the old principal, Joe starts to go down a list of go-o-o-od football players who did play or who could have played in the NFL. Between the two of them, the list goes back as far as the 1940s. It doesn't take long for Epps to nudge up an old tale about B. F. Carmichael, who became the Latta schools superintendent in the 1920s "way back when the earth was young."

The job didn't mean much of an office back then. Carmichael didn't have a secretary. He coached baseball, football, basketball, and girls' basketball. And taught one class. He won a lot of games.

"He carried a big stick, and he would put that stick upon your rind," Epps recalls, chuckling. "He told one of the men backing up his line where to get situated, and that boy slid off about ten feet one way or the other, and when the half came Carmichael took off his belt and cut that boy's rind in two."

Carmichael made his bones coaching baseball by using a knuckleballer as relief pitcher to serve up a no-loss season. The superintendent took his recruiting seriously. He convinced a storekeeper over on the Marion County side of Temperance Hill to buy a bus and drive the community kids to Latta schools, over in Dillon County.

"We could get a baseball team off Temperance Hill," Epps says. "I mean, you'd have to add one or two."

IN THE MOODY HOUSEHOLD it was all about football. Copeland played in a state championship game. Jimmy had been a good player. His brother Randy, closer to Joe's age, was a good player. "All you have is football, football, football around that home," Joe recalls. When the Moody farm was sold, Joe got his chance.

Joe didn't back up from work, his friend Charles Lane will tell you. And he loved the Moody's spreader truck, a heavy-duty dump truck that looks like a cross between a pickup and a tank. Joe would load it up just so he could drive it. Copeland used to say, "That boy would drive it to the mailbox if he could."

It was good for a laugh around Latta High School that Joe drove it to classes. He would work the spreader truck at first light, drive it to school, hop back in, and go back to work at the end of the school day. "From 3:30 to black:40." He once stayed out of school for a week to get fertilizer spread because they were so far behind.

His childhood friends were playing ball too. So the spreader truck took its place in the part of the school parking lot where the football players parked. Some of the other students—and players—considered him a nut case.

"They'd say, that's a fool for you. I didn't care. I was ridin'. My teammates kept ridin' with me on it, hang off the back of it, get down with the fellows back there. They didn't care. As long as they were ridin'."

Joe played guard, offense and defense, there in the middle. How good was he? George Legette, when asked, gives one of those hesitation ahhhs, smiles broadly and says, "He didn't start." Both he and Joe break up in laughter.

SAM CLARDY has a nervous habit of touching his chest with his fingers or wrapping his arms around himself as he talks. He has the pearled eyes of deep faith. He sits propped forward on a recliner in his living room on a hot June afternoon with a decorated plastic Christmas tree up against the wall. He has papers and a Bible spread in front of him. A Methodist minister, he is trying to put together a sermon for the renewal of vows by a couple celebrating their fiftieth wedding anniversary. He's never had to write anything like this before. His hands wave over the papers as he talks about it. Joe calls him Coach.

"He was different than a lot of them," Clardy says, picking slowly over his words. "He didn't have the most talent of anybody I ever coached. He wasn't the smartest. But he gave . . . everything he had." Sure enough, the conversation swings around to the state championship game the team lost on a called fumble that wasn't a fumble.

The story Clardy tells about Joe's grit is how Clardy worked with another teacher to make sure Joe got a passing history grade so that Joe would graduate from high school, because he knew Joe would be a success and he knew he would need that diploma. And it shows, Clardy says, in how Joe's kids have turned out. He jokes about "that Moody fellow" Joe worked for and says Joe kept that farm running for Moody even when Joe was in school.

Clardy used to have a motivational thing for his players during practice. He'd get in their faces and ask, "Are you green or are you brown?" Green was stained with grass, meaning you got down and played. Brown was a turd.

ONE AFTER ANOTHER, Joe's teachers say the same thing: He worked hard. Few of them really know how hard. When football season ended, Joe took a job at the Russell Stover candy plant, third shift.

"Go home, take a shower, get out. Hang in there," he says. He was part of a crew cleaning up the sticky spills of the day's cooking. "Get all that candy off the floor," he says. "We'd throw hot water and mop the floor."

He'd start the job at 10:30 P.M. and sweat it until 6 in the morning, then turn around and go to school. And it's not like he quit farm work all together to do it. So school was tough. English—Joe puffs out a breath and shakes his head to think of it forty years later. He didn't even consider the English 1 class. "That was not my category. I stayed away from that," he says today. He was in the remedial class, contemporary English, where the essential job was, let's get these kids semifunctional before we set them out in the workplace. Because the workplace is as far as they are going to go. It's a wonder he was able to stay awake—and he didn't always—much less graduate. Joe did more. He made his mark. His senior yearbook and memory book are filled with notes from other students. All of them, you realize quickly, are women.

"To: Joe, one of the most sweetest young men I know. I wish you all of the luck in the world, with love, Sharon Lee." In the notes, an English teacher compliments his "quiet manners and soft walk." Must have been an in-joke, you think. But no.

Lou Stoudenmire taught English at Latta High School and taught Joe for his sophomore and junior years. She is a delight of a woman, sharp as a tack. She was raised on a cotton farm in Dillon County and has that bit of a schoolhouse marm to her, with a sweet cackle of a laugh. When she thinks she's taking herself too seriously, she stops herself with a quiet giggle and her voice rises when she giggles.

"Joe was a good boy," she says, then stops herself and blushes a little. "I, I shouldn't say boy. He's still one of my little boys."

Seba Stoudenmire too is an educator, a teacher and then a principal. He is a lot like his wife, courtly and country wise. The couple keep birder feeders among the bushes and flowers in their backyard, and on a summer afternoon the feeders get buzzed by cardinals, blackbirds, goldfinch—and squirrels.

"But I can't tolerate the squirrels," Seba Stoudenmire says. "I run them off. Let's leave it at that. I run them off." And he laughs almost under his breath. He was born in the tiny hamlet of Lone Star over in Calhoun County. The two married in her great-granddaddy's house, where she was raised. "He loves to say he brought me out of the cotton patch and brought me to town," she says with that laugh.

Lou Stoudenmire is one of two teachers, along with the late Millie J. Woodbury, that Joe says he owes his high school diploma to. "If you wanted to learn she would try to teach you. I struggled so hard. She would break it down for you when you were struggling," he says. "Wouldn't put up with no mess."

The kids in Joe's English classes were from all grade levels, Stoudenmire recalls—a lot of them in where they shouldn't have been. Joe was one. "It was no harder for him than it was for most boys," she says. "Most." The formal structure of the language was like a foreign cadence to those who spoke the rhythms of Pee Dee conversation, the rules far different from everyday speech, and the whole parse-and-diagram-the-sentence thing, "well, that was not an easy job for any of them. Young men did not like English. I did everything but sat on my head. You just had to encourage them and make them think they could do it whether they could or not."

But Joe was something more. In a kith-and-kin community like Latta everybody talks, and people talked about Joe's life with the Copeland Moody. The situation was well known among his teachers. The Stoudenmires, like others, admired him.

"I don't know too many people who would do that. I don't know anybody who would have done what you did for him," Seba Stoudenmire tells Joe decades later in an aside that leaves him speechless, for a moment. "We all do what we have to do because we have to do it," Stoudenmire tells a visitor. "Joe went out of his way to do it."

Joe is nonplussed. "I didn't know you knew that," he tells him.

Lou Stoudenmire says she didn't worry about whether Joe would be able to graduate. "I just felt like he was going to do it. He had that in him." She talks about how, despite Joe's less-than-committed approach as a student, the teachers could see the potential in him. He might not have been eager, but he was always willing to learn, she said. That alone was standout. In a time when trouble roiled just under the surface of the newly integrated halls, Joe was never a problem. He was polite, well mannered. A lot of the kids would goof off, in or out of class, just not do their work. Joe "might have fluffed about it some, but I didn't hear it," Stoudenmire recalls, then adds to Joe, "I don't ever remember having to march you down the hall."

MRS. STOUDENMIRE may have been low key, but graduating meant Joe had to go through the crucible: Mrs. Woodbury. His senior year English teacher was no Lou Stoudenmire. Millie J. Woodbury was a take-no-prisoners fireplug who, like Joe, had something to prove. She too was black, working in the newly integrated Latta High School. She wore thick, black-framed glasses with an oval shape that didn't do much to soften her pensive glare. No bigger than chest-high to Joe, she was a scrapper who didn't take no for an answer. She'd smack a yardstick on her desk to get your attention and wasn't above raising it and chasing after you.

Her classes tended to be works in progress. Joe frankly says, "I went to school with some fools." When asked during a lesson, one of his classmates couldn't spell "shoe." He came up with the "s" then began stumbling over letters. Even for the ferocious Mrs. Woodbury, sometimes it was just too much. "She'd hold it as long as she could, then she'd bust out laughing," Joe remembers.

Woodbury would rake her kids over the coals from the moment they came through the door. "Don't tell anybody y'all are seniors," she'd lecture the class. "Don't tell anybody. Tell them you're in fifth grade. Don't get laughed at."

Joe was make-do and seemed unmotivated in class. That wasn't going to cut it. Woodbury too knew about this kid, where he came from and what he could accomplish. She laid right into him. "The diamond's in your pack," she'd tell him, meaning he had potential he didn't show. She got right in Joe's face one time, "right on top of you, you know? 'Son, do you want to graduate? Do you want to graduate your senior year? I hope so. You'll be back in that chair. You'll be right back in it.'"

She told him she sat at home at night thinking about him. He'd walk into class with a pencil propped up on his ear and she'd tell him that was the right place for it, because if he took it out he couldn't do anything with it anyway. "Son, if you'd just give me a little bit," she'd say, holding her thumb and forefinger a sliver apart, right up to his face, for emphasis.

It was tough love, and Joe needed every bit of it. Then he says something that surprises you a little at first. He brings up Angelica, his daughter, who would graduate from the same school as class valedictorian. If Joe had gone to school before he lost interest in it, he says—not bragging but reflective—if he had done that, "I don't think Angelica could hold a candle to me." It takes you aback for a moment, but, judging from the way he went at the rest of his life, it's hard to believe anything less. He did, after all, graduate.

To this day he'll tell you he got that diploma in 1975 but that his class year was 1972. And to this day, the phone will ring in the office of Superintendent Kirby. It's Joe, again. When the schools purchased a property for future use, Joe wanted Kirby to know that if he wanted to rent it to defray costs, Joe might be interested in farming it.

"Joe never calls me to ask for a favor. He's a seed planter. He plants seeds," Kirby says. "Joe's always got a dream, and he has a plan how he wants to do it."

———

JOE GOT INTO one last fight at school as a senior, after all that struggle. A classmate and him, just fooling around Joe remembers it, one of those things where somebody shoves and somebody shoves harder.

"He said, 'I'll take you,' and I said 'You're coming to the bathroom right now.'" They were down on the floor wrestling and punching when a teacher walked in. The assistant principal made it simple for him—three licks or three days. Graduation was on the line, after all that work, all those mornings in the field before class, all that effort just to pass this class, then pass the next. You weren't allowed to be absent for thirty days if you were going to pass on to the next grade. Joe already had twenty-seven days, days he spent around the farm helping Mr. Moody.

"He gave me three licks, and, and, if I'd had a bucket of water I'd have laid down in it right there."

———

JOE WON'T TALK MUCH about the Moodys selling the farm. Today, the land is cut into dirt roads. As you drive down Copeland Moody Road, there's a sign, "Property available/MarCo." Trailers and a few homes surround the old Moody place. That's what Joe sees when he steps out in the morning. The farm didn't have to be sold, he says. The farm should never have been lost.

At the end of his life, Copeland couldn't do much of anything. For a while he made planters out of old sewing machines down at the senior center. Then that got to be too hard on his hands. Joe would bring him around to Aunt Ginnie's, and Copeland would help plant African violet seeds in little cups in her greenhouse. "He was critical and he was sick and he helped put out little sprouts and helped propagate things," Virginia Merchant said. When Copeland could no longer do for himself at all, Joe would take him for long rides in Copeland's '63 Ford. After Copeland was all but confined to a hospital bed in the home, Joe slept on the floor beside him, because he didn't like the cot. Copeland Moody died in 1975.

"Mr. Moody, he was kind of like an infant before he died," Joe says. The last thing Copeland said was to tell Irene to tell Joe to take care of himself. To this day, Joe gets a remote look in his eye to talk about it.

"He was just about like a father to me. I'm going to tell you that for the God's every truth. He was just a man. He didn't care what color a man's skin was, you know what I mean. If he could help him he would help him."

———

THE MOODY ESTATE by that point wasn't much more than the house and a few acres around it. Copeland's will split it four ways in equal shares among Irene, Jimmy, Randy, and Joe. Joe stayed in the bigger trailer out back until he married, in 1981, occasionally bickering with Irene. He recalls one instance where he stood up to her in the kitchen, telling her he was a man and if she was going to treat him like anything else he would just walk out now. After Copeland's death, though, at one time or another, Joe began to eat at the table with Irene.

"Mrs. Moody was there by herself then. It was just, 'Joe, your plate's here, on the table.' So I sat right down and started eating. Eat my food and don't mess with anybody else. I'm not moving my plate over to anywhere else. You know what I mean. So I just started eating."

As one-fourth owner. When Joe married he moved to two acres he bought down the road, across the swampy run and up on a bluff in the pines. The lot was the first land of his own.

♄

Chapter 8

The Money Crop

FARMING IN THE PEE DEE is hit or miss. Lay out a soil map and the land is all mottles. Sand ridges bulge like dunes on top of pockets of richer soil. That's because of the influence of the Carolina Bays, another one of those geological freaks you might not have heard about. The Pee Dee is pocked with them.

The bays are isolated wetlands, basins in the flat coastal plain where rainwater collects and shallow groundwater feeds. They are among thousands on thousands of freshwater wetlands in the coastal Carolinas. But Carolina Bays are oval shaped and tend to tilt southeast to northwest. They seem patterned. Even after years of study, nobody knows how they got there. A favorite theory is that there was a strike by a huge, shattering meteorite or asteroid. But every other alien thing has been blamed, from ETs to huge prehistoric sea creatures mucking around on the bottom of what once was the western edge of the Atlantic Ocean. Some people call the bays whale wallows.

What the bays are is exotics, splotches among the coastal sands where rare plants like Venus flytraps thrive. The surface of some of them is matted with floating bladderwort so thick it looks deceptively like solid ground. The bladderwort, like the flytrap, is a carnivorous bug eater.

The bays can be found from Florida to Delaware, but if you fly over the coastal Carolinas you are astonished: They are everywhere. Or they were. Their eyelid-like outlines can now be seen in acre after acre of cropland. Farmers long ago began plowing into them to get at the rich depositional soil.

It took five hundred acres before you could call your farmland a bay. Joe started with those two acres where he later put the trailer, down the dirt road from the Moody place, across the bottoms and up the hill. He worked at Masonite making rough trim saws, worked at Coca Cola, then took a job at a packaging company. Twelve-hour shifts in the wood yard. He called it day labor. Then he would get to work. In 1978 he rented nine acres by S.C. 301.

"I went out and put my head on the block. Nine acres of land and $900 and one of those small pop pop pop John Deere tractors. Wish I'd have kept it." He planted eight acres of soybeans and an acre of field peas. "Best acres of soybeans I ever cut in my life."

He was struggling with his life. His mom tells how Joe came by on Saturday evenings and they would talk as he helped plant peas and beans and corn. Joe had gotten involved with a woman who had a baby. He washed and cooked and helped care for the baby. The woman used to sit and watch rather than work with him in the field. He would come in from the field, sweaty and grimy, and she'd say, "You can't hug my neck. You can't kiss me." He'd say, "What's wrong with you? You got a baby. How'd you get that baby?" One night he showed up after work and the baby's father's car was parked at her trailer. "I was too country and not hip enough to be the cool boy. And I come home at eleven o'clock to hug her neck and her baby's daddy is standing in the yard. And I got no use for that." Thirty years later, Joe is harvesting sweet corn he grew just to work a field and giving it to anyone who stops by. He wrestles with whether to give the woman any, goes back and forth as he talks to his mother. He decides he will.

In 1979 Joe met with Gary Turner and got to work on his bay. But not before he met Celeste.

―――――

CELESTINE WILLIAMS is quieter than Joe, very deliberate in her own way. She came home from New York to visit, and the Matchmaker went to work. Ruby Becote is Celestine's first cousin. She has a laugh that sounds like smile and an endearing penchant for telling people whom they would "team up with pretty good." Becote worked at a fiber mill in Darlington, and at that time so did Joe Williams. In the break room she went on and on about her cousin.

"I said to myself, what do I want a woman out of New York for?" Joe remembers. Becote laid Celestine's phone number on the table and told him to give her a call.

"He always liked to meet people. He ain't no stranger to nobody," Becote said. "She just wanted to know if he was a nice guy."

Joe picked up the phone. He is a talker, after all. He found this woman he had never met easy to talk to. They kept talking after Celestine returned to New York. Three months later she came back home. Her baby brother met Joe in Lamar, and Joe followed him to the house.

Celestine and Joe Williams. Courtesy of Cathy Petersen.

"He came to see me," Celeste says. "They said he was tall and I looked at him and he was short." Both of them break into laughter. "He had one of them leisure suits. He had one of them shelled shirts." She didn't know what to think. He walked out to his car, a Malibu station wagon. They went to the movies and went and got a hamburger.

"I started hitting it off with him. He kept talking. He loved to talk all the time. And he worked wide open, farming and working jobs. He loved tobacco, salmon. He loved playing the fool in the house." They married two years later. Joe calls her Celeste, "Celeste like I'm blest," she likes to say.

"He always told me, thanks for getting him a nice wife," Ruby Becote says, her laugh beaming.

———

As hard as Joe farmed, he labored hands-on for the wages to make a go of the farming. He calls them public jobs. He didn't have much choice. He even went back to school.

Little Joe was one year old when Joe got himself admitted to night school at what then was Francis Marion College. A woman who lived down the road from him worked in the admissions office, and his papers ended up in the right pile. He showed up for his first class, Math 101, and lasted a month.

"Oh Lord, I was pinching myself," he says. "Thirty days, thirty days. My, thirty days. Francis Marion. And I got an incompletion." The college experience, though, has had its advantages. "You know something when you get out of there," Joe says, nodding his head sagely. When he's in an argument with acquaintances or especially with somebody at work, he tells them, "I've been to college. You ain't been to college."

Joe got a bigger edge, though, early on. He was employed at Masonite in 1979 when he drove out to Sandy Bluff one day to work some peas with his John Deere. He and the farmer got to talking. The old Cotton Grove plantation— with its wide-open, rich farm fields and pine spreads down along the Pee Dee— had been sold to the Boise Cascade Company for a paper mill. The land is prize. In the plantation's prime in 1934, when most fields would yield a half, maybe three-quarters of a cotton bale to the acre, the Cotton Grove fields yielded three bales. The plantation was some of the best growing land in Marion County. The company was looking to rent acres. Joe wrote the Boise phone number on the back of an envelope sitting on his dashboard. He was twenty-five years old and farming 125 acres at the time. The Boise Cascade land lease supervisor was Gary Turner, who met with Joe out at the plantation.

"Joe was easy going, a very personable person. Always smiling. I never, never saw him angry," Turner recalls. They struck a deal for 110 acres. Turner gave Williams a break on the lease, and then they talked sunflowers. Turner wanted a field plowed and planted for dove hunting. Joe kept twenty to thirty acres aside for it. The next year, Turner leased Joe four hundred more acres. It was half the acreage Turner managed for leases. One day Joe looked around from his tractor and realized he was farming more than six hundred acres. His bay. The farm ran all the way from the highway back to the swamp. He had first set foot on the Cotton Grove land in 1968, driving with Copeland Moody to fetch tobacco hands from the farm to help work Moody's crop.

"Just a little black boy on back of the truck. I never knew that I'd work all that land back in there."

By the mid-1980s Joe was working 1,500 acres combined of Boise Cascade land and other fields—a massive and maybe unmatched amount for someone working largely on his own and holding down a wage job while he did it. He calls the company "Boise Cascade Cooperation."

———

THERE TENDS to be a bond like a handshake in Carolinas farm country. People compete, sure, in a state-fair sort of way. But by and large they watch out for each other. Growers share that field-full-of-crops sense of belonging: They are in it together. Respect isn't a question of whose field is bigger than whose. It's who works hard. Joe learned how to grow in the Pee Dee from more established growers. He learned his secrets to tobacco, the money crop, from J. G. Bryant, the farmer he looked up to, one of the more successful tobacco farmers in the region.

Not that there's not subterfuge. There was a farmer in North Carolina black-eyed-pea country who liked to tell about the year he talked around the feed store about planting peanuts. Jimmy Carter, the Georgia peanut farmer, was running for president, and the black-eyed pea farmer told anybody who would listen that the price for peanuts was going to go through the roof. Everybody went out and planted peanuts. He planted black-eyed peas and made good money because of the drop-off in supply.

So the bond isn't quite a brotherhood. That whole "shiftless" thing permeating racism during the times was pervasive in white attitudes toward black farmers, even among the whites who sweated alongside them. After Joe began working the Boise Cascade acres down that dirt back road to the Pee Dee, and by himself, he would look up to see white farmer after white farmer eyeing him as they wheeled slowly past in their trucks. Those were the years he kept that gun in the tractor. During those Boise Cascade years, farmer after farmer approached Turner wanting a piece of the acreage. He turned them down.

"I could depend on Joe," he would say later. "If I had some more land, I'd lease it to him again."

———

YOU MIGHT EXPECT the old Moody place to look odd, there in a grid of dirt roads and trailers and a few cookie-cutter subdivision-type homes. But it doesn't. The clapboard house looks like it belongs. The other homes look out of place.

Joe bought the home place from Irene Moody when she asked if he wanted it. He was living in the mobile home on the two acres he had bought across the run, "right down the dirt road there." Less than a mile away. Irene Moody was widowed, getting older. Her children had moved on. She wanted to move to Charleston to be close to her sister.

"She talked to her young'uns, her birth young'uns, and they weren't interested, so she come to me."

So Joe moved into the home he had never really lived in, renting to own, in 1983. The price was $25,000. The idea of it would have been staggering to him as a child. Asked what went through his mind when he bought it in 1987, Joe says simply, "Nothing." But later on, he says, "I told Joe, if you bury me, son, if you bury me first—I told Angelica the same thing—this is one piece of property I want y'all to keep. If you don't keep nothing else, you keep this house and this two acres. I'd appreciate if you two always hold to this place here. I say, tell your young'uns the same thing. I told Little Joe, whatever you do, you hold to this place right here. I was raised here. You were raised here. Regardless of what. If hell freezes over, hold to this place here."

Celestine gives the old shack behind the house a tolerant look. "Amazing," she says, "that he could live in a place like that."

————

THE WILLIAMS'S HOUSE is a clutter of papers and books, photographs of their children on the wall. A vintage Aeolian player piano in passable shape is up against one wall, with Angelica's basketball trophies displayed across the top. Asked why he bought the piano, Joe fumbles a little for an answer as Celestine laughs a belly laugh. The question has come up before. He found it in 1979 on the porch of a man in the country who, as it turned out, Joe had gone to school with a few years earlier. Joe was doing some work with a distant cousin when the two drove by the house and Joe spotted this neglected old player piano. Virginia Merchant and her husband restored antique furniture. Joe had helped them with some of that, so he had picked up an eye for an antique. He knocked on the door, Floyd answered, and the two renewed their acquaintance. Joe asked Floyd what he wanted for the piano, and Floyd told him it was out on the porch because he planned to throw it away. So the price was right, $25. Joe took the piano to Miss Virginia, and they went to work remodeling and refinishing. Then he brought a man up from Florence to tune it. Joe ended up with a century-old beauty. But now that he had it, he had to find somewhere to put it; living in the trailer, he just didn't have room. Irene Moody, who played piano, took a shine to it. So the Aeolian stood against the wall of the den when Joe moved in. He didn't play; Celeste didn't play. He eventually gave it to Angelica, his daughter. It hasn't been run in a long time, but if you cranked it up, it would work.

Thirty years after he bought the old player, Joe got his first look at the possessions listed in the estate of Scipio Williams. One of them was that organ and a stool.

———

DOGGEDNESS is the impression of Joe that sticks with you. He's not big and he's not small. He has a workingman's body, with rounded shoulders like a vise grip. He moves with the directness of someone getting something done. His head has been on the block time after time with an ax raised, Joe tells you. "But by the grace of God I moved my head before it came down."

He was just the man to take on a mammoth task like farming 1,500 acres solo, with modest equipment. Not too many farmers would touch that kind of spread by themselves with that kind of gear. And all the while Joe worked a "public job" to make do.

"It's pretty doggone tough," Joe's friend Charles Lane says. "You've got too many irons in the fire. You work like you're killing snakes all the time."

Joe was out of the house before sun-up and back so late that it was a week after Little Joe was born before he held him. He couldn't bear to wake the infant up. Friends would pass him by in the fields on Sunday, wave, and yell that they hoped the parson didn't see him.

"He had a lot of land. He wasn't afraid to jump out on his own," George Legette says. "More than I would have jumped on."

Joe wasn't afraid to take advantage of what he could. He's one of those people who seems to know everybody and everybody seems to know. When there was business to conduct—land to buy, equipment or whatever—and someone didn't know him, Joe would tell them, sure they did. "I'm the only black guy the Moodys ever raised." That's all it took. People would nod and go, "You're that guy?" As an icebreaker, you couldn't beat it. And who he is gave him another, unexpected edge.

"I intimidated a lot of people, not by trying, I scared a lot of people in my day. I have scared a lot of people. You see, a lot of people are intimidated by this speech problem I've got [the stutter]. They think that I'm mentally retarded. And I walk fast, they think that I'm mentally retarded. They thought that dealing with me, and I surprised a lot of people, you know? I surprised a lot of people. Not by my trying to be smart or smartass or anything, you know? But I surprised a lot of people."

In 1988, when Joe bought a fifty-acre farm—fully intact with packing house and the home—from a nearby white family, he was told that one farmer complained that "that nigger is trying to buy up everything." Nearly ten years later, the man still pesters Joe to see what he's up to. Joe doesn't let him down. He recently told the man he was buying a three-hundred-acre farm known to be for sale over the line in North Carolina, just to watch his eyes bug out.

"He was about to drop," Joe recalls. "I won't be buying it. I can't afford to buy it. But I tell him, to mess with him, to mess with his mind. He still worries about me, for some reason. He still worries about me. And I push it."

———

JOE'S A WHEELER-DEALER, Walt Brown will tell you with a wry grin. Brown is an executive vice president at First Bank, someone with whom Joe has done his personal banking for years. Brown is both relaxed and thoughtful, almost paradoxically. He's a man with a casual demeanor and a professional air. He puts on his thinking cap when Joe comes through the door, he says.

"Joe has always got something going. He's always got something going. He's always hustling."

———

Joe had to hustle. No sooner had the last fall crops come in, the corn in September, the sweet potatoes in the last of September—"if you can get around to get it done," Joe says—than the soybeans come in, in October into November. Then the wheat has to go in the ground. Joe's forehead furrows as he talks your way through a year of planting. The relentlessness of it comes across with that mad tap-dance feel of someone who just realized he is standing on a red-ant pile.

"You got that much [land], the whole thing's gonna come at you. You just have to keep to yourself, just try to stay focused. Everything be comin' at you because you're sitting on top of it. You've got to make decisions, then the tractor will break down. You've got down time. All this stuff. You've just got to go there and feel it. It'll rock your brain, I'm telling you. You owe debt. You've got an obligation to meet, you know what I mean? It'll take you to another level, I'm tellin' you now," Joe says.

That's life for a farmer. There's always something to do next, and the longer one thing holds you up, the bigger that next one gets on the list. When crops have to be planted, hoed, or brought in, the snap of a piece of equipment giving out might as well rip through the wallet. The toughest part of the deal always came, ironically, right around Christmas. Joe had to settle his farm loan debts for the year, pull out the paperwork again to file for the next year's loan. That's with the wheat in the ground, planted in November and needing nitrogen to fertilize by early March. You already had a payment to make, in other words. And this was headed into the winter "off" season, into January and February, when "you were coasting," Joe says. But when March hit, "you've got to go." So you already needed money. The wheat was going to have to be fertilized if it was going to make it. The tobacco seedlings had to be started in covered beds or greenhouses. And tobacco, of course, was the cash crop, the source of the profit to pay back loans, even at the modest prices achieved butting up at the market against truckload on truckload from more commercial operations.

Tobacco began replacing cotton as the go-to crop in the region in the late nineteenth century, toward the end of Scipio Williams's life, when the rail line came through and the town of Latta was laid out. The crop made the profits that brought the town into its heyday in the early twentieth century. The years when Joe was coming up and started farming on his own, the 1960s and 1970s, were the beginning of the downslide from the crop's biggest years in the region, the 1950s, according to Prince in *Long Green*. But nearly as much tobacco was still being grown, more than a billion pounds.

It's pretty disturbing to ride today through the city of Mullins—that tobacco hub important enough to get its own railroad spur track when the line was laid through Latta. The city's old railroad depot is now the South Carolina Tobacco Museum. Up the track is a row of derelict old tobacco warehouses, rusting rail-cars pulled off onto side tracks all but abandoned.

And it's telling to realize that by the time health concerns finally overrode tobacco's popularity, tobacco farmers were being heavily subsidized. In 2004, a group of tobacco companies essentially bought out the federal allotment program, or quotas, Prince notes. Now farmers could grow as much as they wanted. Of course, the price paid for the tobacco would drop. To make good, the companies paid off landholders and farmers by the pound over a ten-year period. In other words, they essentially subsidized them, taking away even more of any remaining incentive to grow. Over the decade 2000–2010, public and private payouts in South Carolina alone totaled more than $75 million.

Long before Joe started farming in the 1970s, federal regulations put a chokehold on the acres you could grow to produce crops like wheat, corn, or cotton and began assigning farmers the acres by allotment. Naturally, tobacco was right there in the thick of it. By the time World War I set a match to cigarette smoking, tobacco had taken root as the money crop. Everybody grew it, it seems, and grew as much of it as the land could stand. Prince notes that the local supply stores for farmers preferred to carry credit for tobacco farmers on the books because the crop came in sooner, so they got paid sooner. Tons on tons of the stuff were being grown. But the number of companies that bought it could almost be counted on one hand. It didn't take long for them to monopolize the grower's market.

So, as cigarette sales took off, the cigarette companies kept the counter price down by putting their thumb on the price they paid for the crop. The companies made a killing; tobacco farm country went into the economic pits well before the Great Depression.

Graylyn Mansion, the Winston-Salem chateau of the R. J. Reynolds tobacco company president, was built in the times of the 1929 "Black Friday" crash, when farmers were scraping by on pennies. Prince describes the place succinctly: "thirty-five bedrooms (each with a private bath), fifty telephones, a heated indoor swimming pool, a photography room, a flower-arranging room and a walk-in vault for the silverware." Remember, this was the 1920s, when any number of farm towns in the Carolinas didn't have fifty telephone customers.

Well, the government stepped in to make it right and made a progressive mess of the whole thing—which a half-century later had gotten so bad that Joe would have to muck his way through it just to put a plow in the ground. The first programs were voluntary crop reductions and growers' co-ops. You can pretty well figure how well the voluntary crop reductions worked, with money out there to be made. So the government began paying farmers not to grow, the farm subsidy, a money-for-nothing trade. That trade ran as rapidly as kudzu— the "foot-a-night" invasive species—right over top the crops and gave corporate farms a stranglehold on the markets that thrives today. The next thing was allotments, literally limiting how much of a crop could be grown, to make sure everybody got a fair share of the market. Guess what happened. By the 1970s, consolidation was the trend in tobacco growing, with companies cobbling together allotments to beef up crop yield. This perfectly legal sleight-of-land was called lease and transfer—another of the government programs, of course. Someone who held a modest tobacco allotment could rent that allotment to another farmer in the same county, then plant something else on his acreage. The bigger, more successful farmers could grow more tobacco on more land and profit more.

The rule had been sought by farmers. It was supposed to make things easier for smaller farmers, who were scratching by trying to work allotment fields sometimes miles apart. Farming, like any other kind of manufacturing, depends on economies of scale. You want to concentrate your time, labor, equipment, fuel, and—not the least—fertilizer, rather than waste time and money trailering a tractor ten or fifteen miles down the road between fields. So in the real world of allotments, as Prince notes, the little guy found he could make money from tobacco without setting a seed, much less struggling with a market stacked against him. The big guy found he could continue to make a killing. Instead of just gassing and gassing the depleting land with fertilizers to get as much tobacco as possible, larger operations could simply lease more allotments to plant more tobacco.

Pretty soon the little guy wanted a bigger share and the farm loan guys wanted a juicier return, so land lease prices began to spiral out of control in one of those feeding-on-itself furies. Everybody kept overplanting to keep up—so the crop price didn't. By the 1960s farmers were squeezing crops closer together, pumping in as much as a pound of fertilizer for every pound of tobacco, Prince notes. Agriculture schools developed genetic seed that grew tobacco as tall as a man. The tobacco market was overwhelmed.

In yet another futile attempt to fix the impending collapse, the U.S. Department of Agriculture in the 1960s "adjusted" how tobacco allotments were divvied up, factoring in a calculation of expected pounds of crop. For all the good that did: The expected yield was factored in by the acre, so allotments still were determined by acreage. The federal regulators rated tobacco yield at two thousand pounds to the acre and divvied up those pounds on the basis of acreage per county until the quotas were reached. The bigger farmers, with those superior economies of scale and no doubt the indulgence of the lenders, could make this one work in their favor too. By pulling in more than that two-thousand-pound yield, they could offer five to ten cents more per pound in payment to rent more allotments—and grow more leaf. Five to ten cents per pound, Joe repeats. It was pennies to the big guys. It was the profit margin to the little guys. That's the farm economy he was raised in and competed in all his life. That's what he was up against, year after year.

"Tobacco was the money. But you couldn't get it. You'd offer fifty-nine cents per pound, they're gonna go sixty cents per pound and get it. Sure did." On top of that, by the time Joe was planting, inflation blew the whole thing up. Gas prices went through the roof, fertilizer prices, interest rates on the loans. The price paid for the tobacco crop didn't.

Because black farmers almost to a man ran smaller operations, it became harder and harder to scratch out a living from the "money crop" and other crops. By himself, holding a full-time wage job, Joe could have farmed as many as forty or fifty acres of tobacco if he could have rented it. But in the best allotment years, Joe held allotments to plant maybe half that. Meanwhile, the guy the next field over might be planting 150 acres. "That's how it was," Joe says. "That just how it was."

Because his farm fields were down the road from each other in two different counties and his equipment modest, Joe's biggest allotment year allowed him to plant about twenty-eight acres of tobacco, and that wasn't until 1990. Only by luck and Joe's ingratiating pluck did he get that.

"A white fellow didn't want it, and I was [farming] right there beside it. And this white gentleman decided let me have it." It ended up costing Joe a tractor. Somebody stole it out of the field.

Chapter 9

The Last Plantation

WITH MORE MONEY to be had, the big tobacco growers by the 1970s had turned to harvesting machines. Bulk barns—long windowless aluminum curing barns that look like off-site storage compartments—were built on the bigger production farms. It was the edge of the cliff for the little guy, who couldn't afford either big equipment or the big barns and who had to work by hand, with hands.

Unlike bulk barns, packing houses look like the barns they are, usually two stories high. They have canopy roofs extending out either side to shield the trucks unloading or loading tobacco or any other crop. Livestock are sometimes kept in them too, along with the traditional hay-in-the-loft feed. In either the barns or the houses, tobacco gets hung out on racks and dried by a heater. But in the bulk barns, the tobacco can be racked in tightly and handled by fewer workers. A bulk barn can hold a lot of tobacco, and that's one of those economies of scale. The barns cut in half the labor hours and consequently the number of laborers needed. By 1991, Prince continues, only one in every fifty tobacco farms still harvested by hand.

Bulk barns "took away from the old tying ways," Joe says, the hands-on tradition of tying the tobacco into wads and hanging it out to dry. Those were the ways of the little guys like Joe, and the little guys took a beating. The Pee Dee lost seven of every ten tobacco farms, and because most black-owned farms were small they made up most of the losses. The farmers who hung in there continued to dangle off the short end of the stick.

"Federal agriculture policy and laborsaving science and technology became tools that ruthlessly eliminated sharecroppers, tenants and small farmers," wrote the historian and North Carolina native Pete Daniel in the *Journal of Southern History* in 2007. "The increase in USDA programs had an inverse relationship to the number of farmers: The larger the department, the more programs it generated, and the more money it spent, the fewer farmers who survived."

Then, in the 1980s, the bottom fell out of the sale prices for tobacco. Those were the years Joe got the Cotton Grove acres. And it wasn't just tobacco.

By the time Joe rented those first nine acres, out there by the highway, nearly all the crops that could make a profit were subject to some kind of allotment. For him, allotments were just one more set of jigsaw pieces he had to somehow fit onto his fields to make farming work. He had to work from those pre-set limits to figure out just where he could plant what, instead of working from what made the best farming sense for the land he had. Each "off-season" winter, Joe sat down with pencil and paper to match up crop allotments with the land he would have in the spring. It was all experience and hunches, and it was critical to get it right. He had to do it while trying to nail down loans to pay for it all. You couldn't afford to waste land you were paying for; you couldn't afford to lose crops. You wanted to put your best money crops in your best fields, that whole "light" and "heavy" soil thing. When you rented farmland, the allotments came along with the acres but weren't necessarily tied to them. You could move the allotment crops from field to field—so long as you stayed in the same county. You couldn't move them across county lines, say down the road to one of Joe's other fields. That made sense as a rule, keeping the bigger guys from hogging any more of the pie than they already had. But it was punishing for smaller farmers like Joe, who lived along the county line and farmed nearby fields in both Dillon and Marion.

He had a secret to make it work, though, and the secret—go figure—had to do with fertilizer. Lighter, sandy soil didn't clump onto the fertilizer like heavier soil did, so more fertilizer made its way to the plant. Counterintuitive almost, but the sort of thing you pick up on in the Pee Dee, where you are forced to plant sandier land. It was the secret his farming mentor J. G. Bryant had taught him.

"The lighter the land the better the tobacco. Chew right better and everything. A lot of people put their tobacco on their heavy land, because that's the money crop. But your best tobacco will grow on your lighter land."

Joe loved the challenge of growing tobacco, the art of feeding fertilizer, the constant watch on the crop, the relentless tractor work. Even with the fertilizer, you had to plow and plow and plow and plow—plow until you just couldn't do it anymore, Joe says—to keep feeding oxygen to the plant.

That was just one more chore in the relentless demands of a long growing year. And Joe had them all on his mind when he started allotting his allotments—essentially arranging the jigsaw puzzle pieces like chips in the ante for one more gamble that he could outgrow the bigger guys. Year in and out, he had to get it right just to get where he wanted to be, out in the field on a tractor with a crop in the ground. As farming goes, it was high risk: He competed against farmers better provided for, better equipped, and more likely to get the better crop price. Having to go to work without a loan in hand didn't make it any less nerve wracking. That was just one of the plagues of the black farm-loan scandal.

The USDA started giving out loans in January, and Joe knew he wouldn't get his until March. Just the way of things in those days. So he wheeled and dealed and did what he could to get by until March. Year in and out he sweated his winter off season. Then came the "whole hog" year.

―――――

WHEN JOE STARTED FARMING, federal lenders were the be-all and end-all for the little guy wanting to work a field in the South. In what would turn out to be an irony, Joe got his first loan, for $900, from federal funds set aside as start-up money for minority farmers.

If getting the plow in the ground turned out to be relatively easy, keeping it there wouldn't be. The prejudice was rife, and it was pricklier than picking cotton. From 1981 to 1997, the U.S. Agriculture Department discriminated against an estimated 100,000 small farmers who were black or native. A lot of them were in the South.

The practice, like the mindset behind it, was Jim Crow redux. So, maybe it's funny that the put-down name those farmers hung on the USDA is "The Last Plantation." Or maybe it's not. The practice was sharecropping, Joe's friend George Legette says. You didn't have your own stuff. A few years you might make a profit; the next few years you're in the hole. The discrimination could be as nasty as just being denied a loan. It could be as dirty as the loan officer showing up at your farm, inventorying every last item, giving it all enough equity so you could get money to plant but no more. Joseph Fields, a sea island farmer in the lowcountry, recalled it too well in a 2010 article in *The Post and Courier* of Charleston. "Every sweep, every harrow, every plow, rake, shovel. Everything you had, you had to keep an account. They would come around and put a value on it, even your hand tools," he said. "They gave you enough of a loan to get you started but not enough to operate. You could lose your crop, lose your property."

And a lot of people did. The practice wasn't confined to a single generation. The sixty-year-old Fields recalled that his father had taught him that it took everything you owned to get a loan.

"We didn't have proper insurance; they didn't tell us about it. A lot of programs came through, but we didn't know anything about it. We just had to suffer the loss. I guess, the color of your skin, they just didn't want to give you the money."

———

LEON CRUMP has the rumpling walk and the worn face of a farmer, a soft voice belying the fixed intent in his eyes when he talks to you.

He grew up in Cheraw, South Carolina, a town along the Pee Dee upstream of Latta, near the North Carolina line. It has a mill history that might as well be Latta's and that of a lot of other Carolinas towns, with the names crossed out and changed.

Crump is sixty-four years old. At age eighteen he went into the Army to fight the Vietnam War. He came back with two Purple Hearts and posttraumatic stress disorder that devils him to this day, some forty years later. At times he loses track of what he is saying, has to pause and regroup. He's in analysis, he tells you.

"At my age, at eighteen years old, to go from Cheraw, South Carolina, to Southeast Asia to fight somebody . . . I spent twelve months and twenty-three days in the jungle and laid in holes with bodies three and four days old, you know?"

A rage over the injustice roiled through him, and it would carry him indignantly through the next decades of his life. It roils through him today. Nowadays, Crump is the state director of the Federation of Southern Cooperatives, a lead organization in South Carolina working with farmers on the farm-loan scandal payouts. His office is his home, and out back he has chickens and turkeys in pens, beehives back by the edge of the woods. He shows off one of those ingenious contraptions, a hydroponic plant bed made out of not much more than a barrel, plastic piping, and rain gutters. In the barrel he's raising tilapia, the simple white-meat fish that is appetizing even to a lot of people who don't necessarily like fish. A pump from the barrel pushes the water up through the piping to run down the gutters, where he's set cups of pebbles and seeded lettuce and other vegetables. In other words, he's growing the plants hydroponically from the nutrients in the fish water, while the process cleans and aerates the water to return to the barrel for the fish. He's working with farmers to teach them how to grow more with less, helping to prod them into the new world of specialty crops and community-sustained agriculture.

In the early 1980s, still shell-shocked from the war, Crump began working with his brother on a thirty-two-acre farm in Marlboro County, wanting to grow vegetables and raise hogs. When he returned from the war, he had worked with Rural Advancement, the Pittsboro, North Carolina–based farmer's support organization that was in the forefront of battling the scandal, writing appeals for farmers denied loans. So he understood how it all worked. That didn't help.

Both his brother and he had heard the stories about discrimination in the loans. But he knew what loans were there to be had, loans that farmers in the Cheraw community hadn't known to apply for. He expected a fight. He didn't care. He knew what he knew. He saw white farmers getting big tractors and trucks, four-wheel-drive farming trucks rigged out with dog baskets in the back and geared up to take way back in the bottoms to hunt. Nobody in his community was getting anything like that. The deal for them was raw from the beginning. The loans were 80 percent-20 percent. You had to put up 80 percent in equity to get a 20 percent loan. You had to sell the farm.

Meanwhile, the people lending you the money were also controlling how much your farm was valued at. They could dance the numbers until the numbers stacked up against you. The only number they couldn't control, really, was the crop price. That was the ante the farmer could put on the table, while bets were being raised all around him. To catch up, the farmer had to cut what costs he could, say by using less fertilizer.

Ultimately that was digging yourself deeper into the hole. Less fertilizer meant smaller yield. If the fields didn't yield enough crop to make the payment, the lenders came after you.

"When we started out with this, they could take all the collateral you had, even if you had a $15,000 loan or a $20,000 loan and you had equity that was $100,000 or whatever, they could take it all," Crump says. "And that meant you couldn't go anywhere else to borrow money because your property was all tied up."

Nowadays, after the farm-scandal "reform," the lenders can take back only 150 percent of the loan, Crump says. He says it and even he has to stop and laugh at that one. Only 150 percent.

"But that's better than taking all." Then he stops for breath and fixes that intent eye on you. "It should be an equal match, money for collateral."

Not for his brother it wasn't. His brother had fallen behind by the time Crump joined him. So Crump went down to the Farmer's Home office. He waited to hear the agent talk loan services and options, benefits white farmers were getting that black farmers weren't. Loans could be deferred up to five years, to give a farmer time to recover from a bad crop year or two. A family member could purchase the loan or purchase the farm to give the debtor a cash flow.

The options weren't mentioned, so Crump brought them up. That didn't accomplish anything but getting the agent mad. No, they were not going to give his brother any options, even though his brother owed only $15,000.

"And I know people were getting hundreds of thousands of dollars," Crump says, fixing those eyes on you. He and his brother were riding past farmers in towering, air-conditioned tractors bought with federal loan money that a season's growing couldn't possibly repay, and the Crumps couldn't get a loan extended.

"They actually sold the farm at the courthouse steps and had somebody there bidding it up so we couldn't buy it back," he said. "I knew what they could offer us, and they didn't offer any of that to us. And so by them not doing that, I said, 'Yeah, I'm going to tell everybody. I'm going to tell everybody.' So people started coming to me, and I started becoming an expert in how to work through the process."

———

CRUMP NEEDED to be an expert. The U.S. Department of Agriculture was so infested with this stuff that in 2003 it was forced to create an assistant secretary position just to deal with it. Six years later, the federal General Accounting Office gave Congress a report on just how well that worked. The report opened by telling legislators that the new secretary's "difficulties in resolving discrimination complaints persist." It blamed that on the use of bad data, on taking steps to fix the problem that made it worse, on a failure to add diversity to its own field office, and even a failure to properly determine ethnicity—field officers were doing it by sight.

The GAO report concluded bluntly:

USDA has been addressing allegations of discrimination for decades. One lawsuit has cost taxpayers nearly a billion dollars in payouts to date, and several other groups are seeking redress for similar alleged discrimination. While ASCR's policy is to fairly and efficiently respond to complaints of discrimination, its efforts to establish the management system necessary to implement the policy have fallen far short. For example, both we and USDA's OIG have observed that ASCR does not have oversight and control over its inventory of discrimination complaints—controls that are vital to effective management. Despite the numerous past efforts to provide this office with constructive analysis, including recommendations to set timeframes for resolving complaints from beginning to end, significant management deficiencies remain. Such resistance to improve its management system calls into question USDA's commitment to more efficiently and effectively address discrimination complaints both within the department and in its programs.

Whew, that's a mouthful, acronyms and all. Want to really appreciate just how pathetic the USDA effort was? The report noted that after four year, the new Office of the Assistant Secretary for Civil Rights (ASCR) had a $24 million budget and 129 staffers. The one former field officer in South Carolina that Crump said might talk about what happened said he couldn't and that the request needed to be directed to the Secretary of Agriculture.

By that time the Ag Secretary's Washington office was fending off the whole smelly mess, because it had ended up in the laps of people like John Boyd. Boyd is a Virginia livestock and poultry farmer, the fourth generation of a proud family of farmers who pulled themselves up by their bootstraps. When he went to get his loan, the loan officer tore up the paperwork in front of his eyes, tossed it in the trash, and told him when he came back the next year it would be processed the same way, Boyd said. Sell the farm to your neighbor, the officer told him—a white man who already had his loan. Get off your lazy ass and go to work milking those cows for him.

Boyd went to work all right. He organized the National Black Farmers Association, marched on Washington with fifty other disenfranchised farmers, carried a petition to the United Nations. Others were fighting the fight too.

Working with the Black Farmers and Agriculturalists Association, Tim Pigford, a Cumberland County, North Carolina, corn and soybean farmer, filed a discrimination suit that was merged with a second suit to become the "landmark" *Pigford v. Glickman* case. Glickman was Dan Glickman, a trial attorney and former U.S. Representative with extensive experience in agriculture issues, who had become the Secretary of Agriculture. Don't bother even bringing up the David versus Goliath analogy: It would take more than hurling stones to bring this giant down. The suit sought blanket mediation to cover losses for approximately two thousand farmers who could show that from 1983 to 1997 the Ag Department had discriminated against them on the basis of race and failed to properly investigate complaints. Whoa, you think, that is milestone. If only.

The Ag Department pretty accurately saw the suit as the first boulder rolling in what amounted to an avalanche and agreed to look at settling it. But the Justice Department said no, no, each case had to be investigated, one by one—by the department charged with failing to investigate them properly the first time. The farmers' attorneys said, let's go to court. A judge agreed to the class-action suit. The Ag Department then settled. There were two ways to collect: Take a flat $50,000 payment or make a larger claim. Fair enough? Well, to start, the payments weren't cash; they could be loans or tax write-offs. To qualify for the $50-large, you had to present "substantial evidence" that your treatment was less favorable than that accorded a nearby white farmer in similar straits. So you can see where this is starting to go.

One of the subtleties about intolerance in the civil rights-era Carolinas is that it's not particularly intolerant. Until push comes to shove, people tend to live side by side and leave be, so long as everyone stays put. People dump on each other much as a way of saying, "better'n you." It's not just that whites look down on blacks; people who live over here look down on the people who live there. Part of what makes you you is that you're not ignorant like them. So, the farm loan discrimination wasn't just a slap at black farmers, though they took some of the worst of it. The back of the hand was shown to anybody the lenders looked down on. They took care of their own—that is to say, the people who were their own in their own minds. When the chance came to be included in the lawsuit payout, Joe did it with disgust. The thing was wrong on top of wrong on top of wrong. There were poor white farmers he knew who had taken that back of the hand from lenders, just like blacks and natives, he said. "They should have qualified for the money too."

Meanwhile, for bigger payouts you had to prove specific damages for specific amounts. And for either payment option, you had to plead your case to an appointed arbitrator—within 180 days. You can almost hear the Ag attorneys breathing sighs of relief.

But nobody else came away happy, including legislators who railed on about fraud, and some eighty thousand other farmers who believed they should have qualified for the payout. Boyd waged a media war. His association battled for most of a decade to get the dug-in-at-the-heels Ag Department to release records that should have been forthcoming under the Freedom of Information Act. The ensuing suit was filed on behalf of fourteen thousand farmers who could prove they had been railroaded into missing the deadline. The lawsuit was settled for $1.25 billion in 2008—money a contentious, gridlocked Congress was in no mood to go find. That year, the nation spun into the Great Recession. In 2010 most of those fourteen thousand farmers who hadn't died were still waiting to see a penny, and critics were railing on the settlement as a shakedown of the American taxpayer. A shakedown. The hypocrisy here is too thick to drip.

———

To JOE it was "forty acres and a mule," another version of old unkept promises. And, sure enough, when that first round of tax credits was won, most of the Pee Dee farmers didn't get one. The feeling was that the few farmers who did made up stories to make sure they were first in line for the payout.

When Joe went to pick up the paperwork to file his claim, the man in the office made reference to that old "forty acres and a mule" promise for freedmen. Under the proposed settlement, the man said, farmers would get five hundred acres and fifty mules and it would bankrupt the Farmers Home Administration. Joe just stared at him.

"And I said, 'Well, what do you think caused me to file bankruptcy?'"

———

"MOST OF THE BLACK FARMERS should have gotten their money," Crump says about the settlements. "The test shouldn't have been that great. If you went in there and borrowed money, and you were behind on your loan, the debt that you accumulated should have been written off, and they didn't do that. They didn't write off the debt for some of the farmers. They had something called a Shared Appreciation Agreement. That was where they wrote down some of your debt, and what they'd do is, in [so many] years they'd come back and re-appraise [the farm]. If your property increased in value in that period of time, you would pay half the money of the increase."

The debt write-off, in other words, worked a lot like the loans themselves did—"every sweep, every harrow, every plow, rake, shovel." They sized it all up, then told you how much they thought it counted against the money you owed. One farmer Crump knows fought back twice against an appraisal that he thought didn't deduct enough from his loan. He knew his farm was worth more than they were saying. They came back a third time throwing heat.

"And this is what they said now, they said, 'THIS is going to be the last appraisal.' They told him like a child. The man is almost eighty years old. He said, 'OK.' The appraisal came in cheaper than all of them."

A lot of what you need to know about the Shared Appreciation Agreement is summed up in the middle of a fifty-page legal review by Susan A. Schneider, printed in the *Drake Journal of Agricultural Law* in 2002, after she had determined that nearly twelve thousand appreciation agreements had been contracted between farm families and the Farm Service Agency. It reads, "The story of these farmers and the interpretations of the SAAs that they signed reveals a lack of foresight on the part of the government, naivety on behalf of the farmers, and disturbing inequities."

How pervasive was this whole stink in the Pee Dee?

"Around here it was hundreds of farmers who came to me, phone calls daily," Crump says. "This [parking] lot be full."

———

FOR LONGTIME FARMING FAMILIES, this stench was an all-too-familiar one. The lenders weren't doing anything that hadn't been done around these parts for a hundred years or more. In the days of Scipio Williams it was called the crop lien, a practice that would culminate in Jim Crow.

Just as Lincoln had almost certainly surmised, things were Very Different in South Carolina after the Civil War. Reconstruction was in place, with federal troops and assorted managers and thieves overseeing the whole imbroglio. Former slave owners were by and large destitute. A silent majority of the workingman white population had been decimated on the battlefields. The reconstituted state legislature was dominated by former freedmen and slaves. They were roundly depicted as moronic and corrupt—and there was no small dole of corruption—but one of the big reasons for the reputation, the historian Walter Edgar notes, "was not that black politicians had been inept but that they had been effective."

The other reason, Edgar points out, was simply that there were a lot of freedmen out there. A lot. In the lowcountry they outnumbered whites. Even in the Upstate, where whites outnumbered blacks, blacks still composed a sizeable bloc of the population. Marion County, where Scipio lived, was an oddity in that the numbers of blacks and of whites were pretty much the same.

Around the state, the disinherited and displaced ground their teeth, feeling they had been robbed of their very heritage—a mood that permeates some quarters today, a century and a half later. A book that still gets passed around in the lowcountry is *The Prostrate State*, written by James S. Pike and published in 1874. The book's champions are quick to point out Pike wasn't a Confederate. He was a Yankee—and he was on their side! Under the guise of writing an independent assessment of what had gone wrong in South Carolina, Pike lay right into the predominantly black legislature for what he calls barbarism: "In the place of this old aristocratic society stands the rude form of the most ignorant democracy that mankind ever saw, invested with the functions of government. It is the dregs of the population habilitated in the robes of their intelligent predecessors, and asserting over them the rule of ignorance and corruption."

Pike, of course, wasn't taking sides: "It is the slave rioting in the halls of his master, and putting the master under his feet. And though it is done without malice and without vengeance, it is nevertheless none the less complete and absolutely done." Within pages, though, he snidely conceded that "the old stagers admit that the colored brethren have a wonderful aptness at legislative proceedings" after comparing the brethren to parrots and monkeys. This stuff still gets passed around.

Pike went on to detail the dollars being pocketed, brusquely excusing white participation. His conclusion, though, is riveting: "The truth is, that the largest half of the population of South Carolina live to-day in huts and hovels, so poor that their total destruction, from one end of the State to the other, would not diminish the taxable values of the State one-tenth of one percent. They are worth no more than so many dog-kennels or pigsties."

Naturally, he had a solution: "Philanthropy could hardly find a more praiseworthy field for its exertions, or one more likely to repay them in material returns, than to establish a model plantation in South Carolina."

In other words, a virtual return to the slave days, except you pay them. Pike was preaching to the choir. Sharecropping, the "model plantation," was already in practice. And that was the best of what was.

ENMITY RAN blood hot. By 1882, after the federals had left and whites largely regained control of the laws, lynchings of blacks for the "rape" of white women had become tacitly sanctioned, and an accusation was enough to get a man tied to a tree. By 1889, Walter Edgar notes, *The Charleston News and Courier* was reporting, "The condition on the part of the whites is one of absolute safety; on the part of the blacks it is one of utter demoralization." What started as roving bands of vengeance-makers coalesced into the Ku Klux Klan.

Marion seemed to have been peaceable enough. In 1871 the feds put it on a list of South Carolina counties in rebellion, but pretty obviously in error. It was quickly removed and replaced by Union County, in the Upstate. Most of the KKK violence was reported in the Upstate, where whites significantly outnumbered blacks, Edgar notes. But dread bled across the state. A politician in Williamsburg County, just south of Marion, noted in 1870 that he couldn't speak publicly without having a guard.

A century later, Joe was walking home one night after fetching Geraldine a twenty-five-cent pack of Winston cigarettes when he looked up at a passing car to see it full of men in white hoods. Across the road behind them was a cemetery.

"I broke camp," he says, sprinting off through a cotton field in the dark.

In 1869, a state militia had been authorized, essentially a home guard for freedpeople. And Marion County's militia roll included that listing of a Scipio Williams. Gunfire sputtered across the region. Edgar, in the exhaustive history he wrote of the state, says the militias were formed in response to KKK violence. But there's no real denying that the shows of force had to do with frustrations on both sides about just who was in charge—or, maybe more tellingly, who worked for whom. A lot of freedmen were without land and began working farms as laborers or sharecroppers. The difference between the two was plain: A sharecropper essentially leased the land and was responsible for his own crop. He was in charge and could do things his own way. A laborer was little more than a wage slave, and a lot of them weren't treated any better than slaves. The landowners, by and large, wanted laborers. For newly enfranchised freedmen, that just wasn't going to cut it. In *Long Green,* Eldred Prince writes about reports in the Pee Dee of laborers breaking contracts, refusing to work, and deserting the farms. In Kingstree in 1866, he writes, three hundred freed people gathered to demand land of their own. That was the beginning of the organized militias, he contends.

Edgar says KKK. Prince says land. You'd be in denial to think the two weren't related. If the hostility was so intense over who worked whose land, imagine the angst and fears of the few freedmen who owned their land. Scipio Williams's "farm laborer" listing on the 1880 census was just a hint of it. Kingstree is some fifty miles from where Scipio Williams's farm stood.

———

IN 1866, the percentage of black farmers who owned their own land would have been very small. The 1900 census reported that for Marion County the figure was only 20 percent, Prince notes. A lot more were renting land or sharecropping. Even allowing for the hedging of wary freedman "laborers" like Scipio Williams, that's not a lot of ownership.

In 1876, when the federal presence in the state began pulling back and whites took over again in the legislature, the worthy gentlemen dropped the crop lien law on the table. The law seems mundane enough: It gave lenders, mostly country store owners and brokers, the first handout when the crops came in and a farmer had to pay his debts. It was a way of ensuring that debts would be paid by newly landed or sharecropping farmers.

That's just good business, right? Except, first in line meant before the farmer himself. Then as later, the lenders were the same people who decided how much they were going to pay for your crop. They could take you for more than you were worth—and your equity was your land. These were the "forty acres and a mule" days, when under the federal Freedmen Bureau at least a few blacks had been given modest acreage to help them make a go of it. The crop lien abuses were so egregious that a year after the law was passed, the legislature had to rework it to give landowners a little more leash, and the next year it was revised again to give them more leash. This wasn't out of the goodness of the legislators' hearts. No sooner had the crop lien law taken hold than cotton prices began to tank and farm acres began to disappear. Cotton was the money crop then, pretty much the muscle of what there was of a state economy. Everybody had turned to growing cotton, to the point that food supplies became short. When cotton tanked, everybody was left holding an empty shopping bag.

Within little more than a decade, the percentage of farmers who owned their own land dropped from 50 percent to 38 percent, Edgar notes. The average farm size dropped from 143 acres to 90 acres. The collapse was so pervasive it makes you wonder how Scipio Williams not only held it all together but bought and farmed more land while doing so. He made his wealth while this was going on.

Scipio wasn't immune. In that 1898 bill of sale in the Letters Testamentary, he puts himself on the line for $20 per month to buy those 128 acres. That's more money per year than an awful lot of people could make, much less spend. Scipio apparently figured out how to deal with how it was for him. That's what Joe did too. Until the drought years.

Chapter 10

The Whole-Hog Year

THE CAROLINAS tend to swing from wet to dry, a phenomenon that meteo-rologists like to claim is the El Niño/La Niña cycle. When waters in an area of the Pacific Ocean cool down, it creates La Niña: The colder waters stir up winds that prod the jet stream, pushing weather across the United States in a way that tends to leave the Southeast drier.

Ironically, the same winds tend to pull away the high-altitude wind shear that tears apart hurricanes in the tropical Atlantic. So in La Niña years, the Southeast also is more likely to be smacked with a tropical cyclone—a double whammy. Sure, tropical storms mean rain. But not the rain you want.

Tropical cyclones tend to blow through in late summer into fall, too late to do anything for the crop except flood the harvest. The rains are not the steady soaking winter rains farmers crave. They're raging freaks, the sort of hit-or-miss monsters that can pop a few drops in one spot while dumping a foot of rain a few miles away, drowning a ripe crop in that field. In Summerville, South Caro-lina, in 1999, a thundercloud poured nine inches down on a few neighborhoods in little more than four hours at high tide, when the full-tide Ashley River was too swamped to drain. Low-lying streets flooded two and three feet deep. The real freak here: The downpour wasn't from an immediate tropical storm; it was from a remnant cloud of a washed-out Gulf tropical storm that was moving across the state. The thunderhead stalled when it hit coastal winds, sat overtop the neighborhoods, and let loose. The deluge was so local that people who lived a few miles away had no idea what was happening.

———

IN THIS KIND OF FREAKISH CLIMATE, irrigation is the sole steadying hand. Without it, a farmer is gambling by guesses. Now, that's not so bad: El Niño/

La Niña patterns tend to prevail for months if not years at a time and are slow to transition. So the weather you see in early spring is a pretty fair indication of what you might face in the summer. A good soaking winter is every reason to plant aggressively. But you're guessing.

The early '80s were drought years, and Joe took some heavy losses. By 1985, astride that tractor running more than a thousand acres, with no real affordable way to irrigate, he was struggling to keep the wheels under him. In 1986 extreme drought strangled the state. It dried up farm ponds, killed unirrigated crops. The agriculture economy skidded into recession, and farmers in the Pee Dee were deer in the headlights.

Crop prices had been good, and land prices had been going up. Farmers traditionally use land equity for loans to finance everything from seed to tractors, not to mention the purchase of more land, so they did. The money people jumped at the chance to do more business. Everybody started speculating, and land prices kept climbing. It was an eerie sort of dress rehearsal for the suburban real estate boom that blew up in everyone's face two decades later—just as tobacco was for Black Friday in the 1920s. In fact, if you really want to get a crystal-ball read on what's going to happen in the investment world, keep an eye on agriculture.

"Joe got overextended. That happened to a lot of folks," Walt Brown, the banker, said. "The price of the land was inflated significantly, by speculators, farmers, and everybody. Lenders. And the utility value, which is what you can produce—that's the true value in my mind—just wasn't regarded, and it collapsed. When the market value is way beyond the utility value, it just doesn't work."

Joe's view of it is a lot simpler, naturally. And just as telling.

"We had some bad years in there, years in the drought. Dry years. And we got in the red. And it just started dying out," he says.

Joe was borrowing to hold together the planting until he got his USDA loan; then he was borrowing from USDA to plant. In 1986, he couldn't pay it all back. In 1987 he declared bankruptcy to give himself a chance to climb out of the hole. Then he got back on the tractor. "We kept farming," he says about it. "We kept farming."

———

In 1989, Joe put it all on the line. "The whole-hog year," he will tell you. He had bought the fifty-acre Turner farm, giving him for the first time his own packing house on site, as well as a storage barn. So he bought the supplies and prepped to plant all of it—every last one of 1,500 acres. He would put in twenty acres of the tobacco money crop, fifty acres of sweet potatoes and watermelon, seventy-five acres of corn. And all the rest in wheat and soybeans.

"Eighty-nine was the year. It was a good year. We just turned the water faucet on when we needed rain," he said. By the end of the year he'd find he couldn't turn the faucet off fast enough.

————

Now, rotating crops is a given in good farming. You put some of the land in money crops, put some in crops that will reintroduce nitrogen or nutrients when they are turned back in, and leave some fallow, moving from field to field in a rotation to keep the soil as fertile as possible. But when you have loans to pay off, the pressure to overplant is intense, and fertilizer makes it worthwhile, for a while. Joe isn't shy about saying he cheated on the rotation sometimes, looking to get the most out of the best of his land.

In a small farm operation, tobacco is a lot like cotton—hands-on and labor-intensive. Even picking the crop means making a leaf-by-leaf judgment about what's ready as you work down the row. In May you're hoeing the grass out from the plants. In June—at the same time you're cutting wheat—you're "suckin'," working hand over hand to pull the flowers, or "suckers," off the tobacco plant.

Regardless of the health issues surrounding tobacco, it is a beautiful plant. The rich resins smell is so sweetly intoxicating that, while following a truckbed of golden leaves down the road, you can't help but roll down the window and savor. For generations, the heaped-up loads on the trucks and that smell made for one of those nowhere-else moments in the Carolinas. And the clusters of fluted white flowers that bloom on the plant are as slender and graceful as wildflowers. But for a farmer the flowers are trouble. Tobacco is sold by weight, and the plant's moisture is its weight. The flowers, Joe will tell you, suck it dry.

Then you have to bring in the tobacco by Labor Day, to compete for the best price. In a normal growing season, the big commercial farmers had their combines out in the field harvesting by August, and Joe wouldn't be able to get to his until September, as the last of the watermelon was coming in.

For the smaller farmers, bringing in the tobacco still meant stropping, or stripping the leaves, one by one, by hand. The traditional way, the way Joe had grown up. You picked while at the same time sorting the grades of leaf for market as best you could, bent over and achy, as you worked your way down the row. Joe preferred to strop his own crop, relying on his own eye to sort grades. But the demand to get the crop in meant hiring harvest laborers. The bigger farms, meanwhile, were running those combines. The labor, in Joe's words, started migrating elsewhere.

————

JOE WAS in whole hog, all right. He was still in bankruptcy, committing himself to an all-or-nothing effort to wrest himself from debt. It was a massive gamble that would mean working day and night, day and night, a relentless pace even by his standards.

"Young. Crazy. You just done it. You go," he says two decades later. Want a glimpse of just how crazy? The day Joe bought the Turner farm, he refinanced his bankruptcy to bring the payments down, partly to be able pay for it.

The Turners were old friends of the Moodys, people who had known Joe since he came to stay with the family. They were close enough that when Phillip Turner died, Joe went to the funeral. The land was good soil. Turner had a tobacco allotment. The place was immaculate.

"He come back and see how that place looks now, he'd come up and start choking me," Joe says with a smile twenty-five years later. "Everything had to be neat, the barn shoveled, painted, and everything. He would have a fit if he'd seen that place looking like it's looking now."

Joe knew Betsy Turner was going to sell.

"The farm come open right there at my door, and I wanted it. It only stayed for sale for one hour. I bought the option on it," Joe says. He managed that by putting the farm in Celestine's name because she wasn't in bankruptcy, then selling twenty-five of the acres to his brother-in-law.

Asked if he wasn't worried about taking on that much additional debt while already in bankruptcy, Joe says, "Sometimes you go with . . ." And he stops and laughs. "Well, it worried me." But it didn't stop him. "I worked a twelve-hour shift that night, meet at the lawyer office that morning at nine, closed the loan up. Got a guy to drive me to Columbia. I slept on the way there. Meet with the bankruptcy judge. Then at seven o'clock that night I was back in the paper mill. Ain't that weird?"

————

LATTA IS ONE OF THOSE fewer-and-fewer places where the closest things you find to nationally recognized franchises are the IGA food store and the dollar stores. The name-brand chains, the Wendy's, the McDonald's, aren't in town. They're out where the business is, along I-95, right there by the fireworks stand.

So, maybe it shouldn't be, but it's a little surprising to stand on the hot asphalt outside an area bank with sweat trickling down your back and watch the cars come in—the old beaters, sure, the tricked-up trucks and hot rods. But among them like a shark glides a brand new Mercedes and not the little one. Then an out-of-the-showroom Lexus. Not the sort of machines you associate with a country farming town.

The old money in the Pee Dee is largely held by a few handfuls of families whose pasts have one thing in common—cotton gins. The powers that be.

When they said cotton was king in the South, they meant it. It's no coincidence that any number of today's banks and brokerage houses began as cotton brokers. The brokers were gin operators who became profitable enough to hold sway, a lot like a mill owner in a mill town. Farmers depended on cotton-gin operators to buy the crop, so an owner could operate a virtual company store, handling everything from selling fertilizer to warehousing tobacco. And making loans. If you wanted a good price when you sold, you wanted to be in business with the buyer.

Cotton-gin operators became the seed store, the hardware store, the market, the shipper, the works. The owners paid farmers for their crops with bank notes or their own promissory notes, which local businesses and even the banks had little choice but to redeem, with so much broker money on their books already. Any number of prominent South Carolina names appeared on those notes. The brokers effectively became banks. They owned the place.

The system wove its way so far into the culture of everyday life that even today, with cotton no longer a go-to—or sometimes even a profitable—crop, small-town farmers still go to cotton brokers, no matter what they're farming.

Copeland Moody ran a small fertilizer warehouse, maybe just so he didn't have to deal with the bigger operators. He knew as well as anyone that when you dealt with the Big Guys, they could end up holding the pot. The fertilizer in Copeland's warehouse was brand name, not so different from the other brand-name fertilizer warehouses competing down the same street on the rail line. A fertilizer company, in fact, originally built his warehouse.

In a lot of ways, the old Moody Agri Co. warehouse looks like the big brother of the trailer Joe moved into. It's sheet steel set up on cinder blocks, hand-built for function. It's oblong, running little more than the length of a good-size house. Inside is a single storage room with a tiny office on one end. It has that "good 'nough" feel and is not nearly as impressive as the broker buildings up the street.

For operations like Copeland Moody's, the specialty was service, carving out a relationship with each individual customer, working to his needs. And spreading for him. The reason Joe could get away with driving that spreader truck all the time in high school was that, when you bought the fertilizer, warehouse workers brought it out to spread. The trains would offload the fertilizer right at the warehouse bay doors on one side, and the trucks backed up for it at the bay doors on the street side—those doors where Joe can still point out the dents he left.

"I spread fertilizer before I went to school and loaded up when I got home," he recalls.

The train passes by so close that the deep, descending screech of its whistle vibrates through you like a huge car horn passing. The train comes so close you feel the locomotive pant.

"This place used to jump now," Joe says. "The railcar used to come off over there where you'd get in line."

The fertilizer warehouses competed with the cotton brokers, who tended to sell fertilizer they had mixed themselves and that could sell a little cheaper than the competition if they wanted. So the business was pretty cutthroat. Warehousemen like Copeland Moody made it work by spreading the fertilizer cheaper than the competition. That was Joe.

It was all about keeping your customer. When you lent him money to operate, you virtually owned him. Copeland never talked to Joe about why he ran his bargain warehouse. But Joe suspects he knows. Copeland didn't want to own anybody.

Forty years later, Joe points to the corner of the property out by the intersection, where the gasoline tank stood. He walks to the warehouse wall to look for the Moody Agri Co. sign, which you could still see a few years before. It's been whitewashed out.

The building was "just like you see it," he says. "They took one of the doors off there."

He has tried to buy the place, but the owners want too much money. He's waiting them out. He doesn't have any real use for it. He talks about wanting it as a souvenir. You get the feeling he just doesn't want to let it go.

———

JOE WENT LOOKING for a loan in 1989, and he had little choice. His USDA loans had been piecemeal anyhow—$50,000 for 1,400 acres of land—enough to get started with but not enough to run. Joe says he was told, "You take this and do the best you can. I'm not going to lend you this kind of money." One of the ways Joe had been getting by until the USDA money came and then finding more to make it work was to run tabs for supplies with cotton-gin men in the area. In 1987, Joe's first growing season in bankruptcy, the USDA cut him off. Not a cent of the money he would need to dig his way out. It was a smack upside the head. He began running bigger tabs with the cotton-gin men, money to pay for the entire year. By 1989, he had no choice: It would be cotton-gin men who backed whole hog.

Joe was good business, too good, borrowing to farm more than a thousand acres. He became the first black man in the region, that he knows, ever to pay back a broker more than $150,000 in loans. Most black farmers were borrowing on fewer than a hundred acres, white farmers on only a few hundred.

"First to farm that much land," Joe says. By a long shot. And one broker let him know. He let Joe run the tab, sure, in cut-and-dried farm-loan fashion. He let Joe run a very long tab. The broker had always been good to him, Joe says, giving him fertilizer and other supplies as needed. Now the screw turned.

"He told me now, he said, 'Joe, you're getting too big for me now. When you pay me out every year, I want you to still bring your money up here to me, and we'll manage your money for you.' I said, 'What?' But he told me that I'm going to bring my money over to him. You know I'm not going to do that." The broker was a good man but hard, Joe says. He trapped anybody who was foolish enough to walk into it. Joe had been just hard enough to trade with him. But he knew that, one way or the other, this was the last tab.

"How do you think he got rich? How do you think he got rich? Now one thing about [the man], from what I've seen and heard, he was not prejudiced. He would clean you out, white, blue, or black. He'd get you so where he could take your land, tractors and all. Right. He didn't have no kind of prejudice."

———

THE WHOLE-HOG DEAL quickly went south. In April, with the growing season under way, Joe yanked to lift something hefty, and his back yanked back, spasming in pain.

He had first hurt it two years earlier, pulling sheet metal out of a ditch. It was one of those nagging injuries that just didn't go away, not with him working a full-time job and farming on top of it. This time the pain about bent him over. The doctor told him he had a ruptured disc, and he had no choice. So Joe went under the knife and out on workman's comp after the surgery. But there was no workman's comp for one-thousand-plus planted acres. Joe had a bankruptcy and a chancy loan riding on those crops in the field. So, the farmer who worked for himself hired an overseer to shepherd three migrant workers full time and hired twenty-one more workers during tobacco season, while he stayed up on the tractor. It was a big expense, but this was whole hog. Joe had too much cash on the line.

Then one day a man showed up with a video camera. He told Joe he was surveying black farms, trying to record the customs. He gave him the sense it was a documentary. The oddity of it maybe should have tipped Joe off. But the man spun a good tale. He asked Joe to "prime" a row of tobacco for him "here to yonder"—in other words, pick the leaves by hand, while the man filmed. He got his documentary all right.

"They put a spy on me," Joe says. The next thing Joe knew he was in front of a woman from the insurance company, the documentary maker in the seat next to him. All three were watching video evidence that a man claiming disability benefits for a bad back was out there in the fields, stooped over, farming twenty acres of tobacco. That was grounds for fraud. Joe had been set up, and he had a pretty good idea who did it. "People were running their mouths," grumbling about his drawing benefits while he tried to bring in a bigger harvest than any of them had ever tried. The woman from the insurance company, "She tried to Bogart me," Joe says—a reference to the tough-talking old movie star. "She tried to force a settlement." He got in her face and cussed her.

"You don't know how my back feels," he told her. "You ain't no doctor." He told the man with the video camera, "You come back by my place and I'll blow your damned brains out." But he had to go back to work at the wage job. The back hurts him to this day.

The last stab came in September, late at night. Hurricane Hugo buzzsawed nearly everything north of Charleston for some fifty miles, smashing homes across the barrier islands, snapping most of the pines in the 200,000-plus-acre Francis Marion National Forest. Everyone who ducked his or her way through it has a story to tell, and more than two decades after landfall it takes only a mention for the tales to start flying. There are the famous ones, like the paramedic who lashed himself to an electric conduit on the roof of the flooded Lincoln High shelter in McClellanville, clinging to a three-year-old girl whom a pregnant woman had passed through the ceiling to him and spending a night he described as like death in your face. There are the countless "ordinary" stories—huddling in a shelter in the dark listening as huge things slammed reverberating against the wall outside.

Among the wreckage was Pinckney Estates in Ten Mile near Awendaw, the family community of descendants of the freedman who slipped away to Capers Island to escape being enslaved just before the Civil War, then floated the pieces of his house back across the sound after a 1870s hurricane destroyed it. Hugo blew their houses off the waterfront and left the splinters strewn with furniture out in the yards. For days, the community's only water came from a hand pump dug by seventy-six-year-old Lucian Pinckney behind the piles of wood that had been his home.

———

THE STORM is legacy in South Carolina. Its highest recorded winds were nearly 140 mph, and in the Lowcountry folks will swear winds were much stronger; it's just that the winds tore the measuring devices apart. The monster made landfall just north of Charleston and tore a gouge through the countryside as far as the Blue Ridge in North Carolina before the mountains gassed the heart out of it. Winds were more than 100 mph in the Midlands and still at hurricane strength passing Charlotte, North Carolina, two hundred miles inland. Hugo killed at least thirty-five people and left behind some $6 billion in devastation.

———

LIKE ANY GOOD lowcountry tale, the storm has its ghosts—the appearance of the auguring Gray Man on Pawley's Island or the courtly gentleman in morning coat, top hat, and cane who greeted a reporter edging along a swamped street in the historic district of Charleston, tipping the hat slightly with a "good day" and an invitation to come back.

———

MONSTER HURRICANES ARE EERIE—the power, the pulse to them. The vast wreckage they leave inspires awe until the horror sets in. They shatter the landscape along a plumb line of debris. Then you go a few miles this way or that way and the damage isn't much more than a few trees snapped or uprooted. Then there's no damage to be seen. It's like the way a tornado tears apart a home in its path and leaves homes on either side relatively untouched.

The right side of a hurricane is the worst, the part likeliest to churn up the most powerful winds and tornadoes. Hurricanes whirl counterclockwise as they move. They push the air mass in front of them, creating friction that slows the winds, then recoiling from the friction to spur the winds along. Think of it like this: If you walk uphill swinging a rope with a rock tied to the end, the weight makes it harder to swing uphill, but then the weight of the rock makes it swing harder downhill. So winds coming off the backside of a hurricane—off what would otherwise be the lee side for lack of a better way to say it—are usually the worst of it.

Nearly half the forty-six counties of South Carolina were declared disaster areas in the aftermath of Hugo, and all of them were in the path or to the right side of the storm. One of these was Dillon County, even though most of the damage there was fallen limbs and trees, and the disaster declaration was needed largely to claim federal money to help clean up. The sole Dillon County death was a seventy-six-year-old invalid who couldn't escape a fire that broke out in a house lit with candles. But the night was terrifying. When Hugo turned toward Charleston, the right wall turned to the Pee Dee. It devastated the coast as far as Murrells Inlet, some fifty miles north of Cape Romain, which took the worst blow. Murrells Inlet is about half as far north of where the eye made landfall as Latta. The storm is remembered mostly for ripping apart Charleston and the Lowcountry, then blazing a bee line toward Charlotte. But a storm that big does a lot of collateral damage. High winds tore through Latta too.

"Hugo kicked butt up here," Joe says. "We stayed at the house. We rode it out. And Lord knows, it was rough. I stayed up, had my clothes on, laid my young'uns across the bed. It was pitch-black dark and all you could hear, it was like the roof of the house come off."

They got through all right. A few pecan trees fell, but nothing landed on top of the house. And, remarkably, with trees tearing apart around it, the little travel trailer where Joe first stayed at the Moody house, it just sat there.

———

According to the U.S. Army Corps of Engineers, Hugo wreaked some $294 million in damage to agricultural buildings in the state. At least one of those buildings was a rented barn in Marion County, packed full of Joe's tobacco.

Joe just managed to pull the last bit of the crop from the fields the day before Hugo hit. The winds tore off a piece of the barn roof, rain poured through, and the storm knocked out the power. The tobacco began sweating, moistening, and rotting rather than drying. Joe did what he could, but the loss turned the money crop into a break-even.

Stacking insult on injury, the man from whom Joe had rented the barn received an insurance payout on the damage, Joe says. "He took the money and stuck it in his pocket, and my tobacco was in the barn and falling in rags. It was leaking, raining on it. I paid the premium [with the rent money], and he took it and stuck it in his pocket."

Chapter 11

Legacy

JOE'S BAY is grown in now, scraggle pine, bottom trees sprouting in swamp undergrowth.

"This is where it stops," Joe says, in among tiger lilies and hardwood. "Everything you see in pine were fields, OK? Still. Everything you see. It was a huge farm, now. You'd get back here on a tractor and you'd run a while. I hadn't been back here in a long time. I didn't like to ride back here because I didn't want to see it all grown up like that. Yeah, that was my forty-two-acre field right there."

To this day he wonders if he should have just quit the day job in 1989. He should have just capitalized, he says. Gone at it full bore. He did all right. But if he'd gotten in full time and managed it, he could have been working as many as five thousand acres.

"But God and kids, it might have killed me, you know? You know?"

When he did go back to the plant, they put him to work at the furnace, in 120-degree heat. Even with that he brought in the crop, the whole hog, even though it cost him a lot more than he planned on. The sweet potatoes didn't match up against others grown in nearby fields, but all in all the crops did well. Then it came time to pay up. Joe went back to the broker to settle the debt. It didn't settle well.

"Paid him something like $125,000, $130,000 that year. OK? Got through that year and he's still saying I owed him $19,000. Then he said, 'For the 1990 year, for me to back you, you're gonna give me everything you've got. I want your house. I want your land, your tractors, cows.' And I told him, 'I can't do that.' He was the top man. I liked him. But he'd clean a lot of people out, you got me now?"

———

ALL THIS LEADS to sweet potatoes. In 1990, still in bankruptcy, Joe cut way back and sublet the fields in the bay. And he went to see the potato man. Just one of his frustrations from 1989 was the poor yield from those fifty acres of sweet potatoes. "If I'd have done right by them, I'd have made a pile of money," he says. But he just couldn't seem to bring in a good crop and didn't know what he was doing wrong. The sweet-potato farmers around him were proprietary enough that they weren't going to tell.

It wasn't his biggest frustration, for sure, but it was the one he could do something about. During the whole-hog year, his migrant camp leader had gotten to talking about a man he had worked for across the line in North Carolina. "He said he was pulling in four or five hundred bushels per acre. Taters. Taters. Taters," Joe said. The camp leader had walked away with the potato farmer's buckets. So Joe went to return them—with more than a little trepidation. The sweet-potato man was white, and there was no telling how he'd take to Joe. The man was a piece of work. He was retirement age, but there wasn't any of that in him. He wore overalls everywhere and chewed tobacco so persistently that he had that classic nasty spittle and stain running down the corner of his cheek. He carried a pearl-handled .25 pistol tucked in his belt.

"Cussed every word he said. Worried his wife so bad they said she just ended up committing suicide. Shot her brains out right there in the house. That's what they told me," Joe says.

But go figure. The two farmers hit it off. The potato man "gave me the recipe," Joe says, a method that would enable him to grow some three hundred, four hundred acres of sweet potatoes. Putting the whole recipe in this book would be telling, but Joe will give you a hint. "It takes potash to make sweet potatoes," he says.

Joe was back in business when he bumped into a farmer who worked a field alongside one that he worked. The farmer told him he wasn't going to plant his tobacco allotment that year. The added allotment would give Joe the largest tobacco crop he'd ever planted, twenty-eight acres. The money crop.

"A white fellow didn't want it, and I was right there beside it. And this white gentleman decided to let me have it." Still in bankruptcy, Joe would be taking on another $10,000 in debt to pay for the allotment and farm the field. But he stood to make as much as $80,000. The farmer in him couldn't say no.

"That year really would have been the boom," Joe says, "but the dry grass come." Drought. He barely broke even. "Sweet potatoes need so much water too. And it was dry. You don't get water, you ain't gonna make it. You can't get the gas to go in your car, you ain't going. That's the way it is, you know what I mean. That's just the way it is."

––––––––

THE BOISE CASCADE land was put up for sale in 1994, and before the signs went up Gary Turner came by to talk to Joe about his bay. The price was $1.3 million and the timber on the land could be cut to fetch about half that.

"Could have bought it for a song," Joe's friend Charles Lane says. But Joe was too far in the hole. He couldn't do it.

"If the man had loaned me money to run my operation right . . . it was good heavy land. Heavy dirt. Oh my Lord, there ain't no telling. I might have it all back there by now. I might have bought it." A decade later, Joe takes that wistful drive down the road to his old tobacco bay.

"I wish, Lord, I wish I'd have jumped on it now," he says. "I don't know. Just something that gets in your blood. You're raised around it all your life. And Boise offered me every bit of it. They offered me every bit of the farm land, Boise did. I don't like coming back here. I want to see fields grow. I want to see fields, not woodland."

Later Joe tells his mother. "It sure has changed back there, Ger'deen. God knows it has changed. It's all in trees back there."

––––––––

JOE HAD A CHANCE to buy Scipio William's peg house, back when he was still a kid and too young to really think about it. In 1977, the owner of the property began dividing roadside lots to sell, and the old house still stood on one of those lots. It was two years after Copeland Moody died, while Joe was still living with Irene, about the time he bought those two acres down the road and took the first stab at farming on his own. He was on the hunt for land to work and would soon rent those nine acres down by Highway 301.

But he would drive by and look at the old place. The price was $7,000—a lot of money then for a kid living in a backyard trailer. The lot was a little less than an acre, too small to be of any farming use. But Joe would drive by and look up at his old family home. Thirty years later he can still see it there, in his mind.

"Lord, I wished I'd have bought it. It'd still be there if I'd have bought it. I'd have put a century farmhouse marker on it."

The man who bought the lot tore down the peg-and-stile house and put up a simple, no-nonsense brick ranch home.

––––––––

THE FLASHPAN PHOTOGRAPH of Scipio that Geraldine remembers seeing when she was younger hung in Aunt Lou's house for her life. It's one of those American Gothic sepias of Scipio and Laura, his wife, and Lou posing for the camera. Scipio has a trimmed white mustache and beard, and he peers serenely into the lens, quietly prosperous and proud. Laura looks younger. She stares off into the distance—like Lou maybe a little uneasy with the bright pop.

The resemblance doesn't jump out at you. Joe looks more like his great-great-grandmother than his great-great-granddad. But the more you look, the more you realize his features are a meld of them both. He might have been their child.

Nobody in the family seems to know where the photograph went. But Queen Gordon took a Polaroid of it when she was younger and later transferred the Polaroid to a digital image. For the Williams reunion in 2010, she put it on the cover of a family genealogy she is working on. Along with the picture, Aunt Lou had the furniture her father made, and when she died she left a trunk full of personal items. Other family members handled the estate, and nobody in the family seems to be able to say what happened to the items.

Other than the ghostlike image from the photograph, the most visible reminder today of Scipio Williams is his fields. And Joe, one of the last active farmers among the Williamses, the only family member with a piece of great-great-granddad's land.

––––––

JOE GOT THAT SECOND CHANCE in 1999. The house was gone, but the land was still farm field out behind where it stood. The family that owned most of that old Scipio Williams homestead land put a good chunk of the acres up for sale. Joe ran into one of the family members in an insurance office. The man was well aware of Joe's interest.

"I've got a piece, I think, on Old Ebenezer Road," the man told him. "And I'm selling it off, you hear?" Joe heard all right. "I said, 'My granddaddy, my great-great-granddaddy used to own some land on down there on Ebenezer Road.' He said, 'I think we might be interested in selling that tract of land.'"

Joe thought back to 1977, the old peg-and-stile house, the homestead, the land where Scipio and Laura began what Joe knows of his family and where Aunt Lou stayed after his death to raise her brothers and sisters. He had a title search done on the acreage, right back to the "x" of Scipio Williams.

"That's some of the land my great-great-granddaddy owned, and I sure hope you can sell it," he told the man. The man said he had to talk to family, give him a couple of weeks. Joe knew it was a long shot.

"I didn't really count on it," he says later. "But I said, I hope, I hope it's going to come through." It was every hour of a few weeks before the phone rang. The family had decided to let Joe have the land.

"I like to fainted—46.1 acres of the 384 acres," Joe says. "You got me, now? Oh, man. I know what it is. I knew I was making history. I know what the history is. For ninety years it had been gone." Cash was so tight he had to borrow from a longtime friend to pay the modest earnest money. It's a small thing, but in a way not really at all, that the friend is white. Joe somehow put together the rest of the financing. The day he signed the papers, he went out through the field. "I walked it, looked at it, and I told Grandpa, 'I've got some of your land back here.'"

The thorn in the thing is that the acreage doesn't include the lot where the peg-and-stile house stood, that single lot along the road, where the now-weather-beaten brick house sits. When he plows the field, Joe plows literally around the house. But he doesn't own it.

———

FARMING TAKES its bites out of you. Joe will work his way down his body reciting the list of injuries, from the scar where he cracked his head open on machinery to the ankle he broke cultivating.

———

JOE HAS BEEN with the container company for a quarter-century. Early on he put up with a lot of petty discrimination but eventually won that regard given a veteran employee who knows his job. The place has its own corporate caste system that's pretty familiar to anybody who's worked in a manufacturing plant. You can tell immediately where everybody stands by looking at people's hard hats. White hats are execs. If a white hat heads your way, you'd better straighten up. Yellow hats are the wood lots workers, green hats are the maintenance guys, and so on down the line. In other words, everybody has a place, and everybody else knows his or her place. Joe has been there long enough to have grown a hard groused skin about it all.

"Punching in the clock," he says with a tired edge. "Ain't doing what I want to do." He spends hours up on a bulldozer, pushing chips that have been dumped from a rail car, pushing the piles into the mill. The work is loud, and when he gets off he tends to speak louder for a while until his ears adjust. Coming off one long late night shift, he flexes his aching knees. With another shift due in only a few hours, he decides—uncharacteristically—to leave off farming for the day. "I ain't gonna do nothin'," he says, "Just go home and rest."

Decent wage jobs aren't so easy to come by in the Pee Dee, with its labor force of the undereducated and the relatively underskilled. Mill jobs are mostly hands-on, and any one set of hands can pretty easily be replaced by another. So even in the yards there's elbowing for status and backbiting.

"You try to do your job and there's people who won't do theirs, and they tell everything to make themselves look good. It makes me sick to my stomach," Joe says. That's the way things are in a lot of mills and, really, any work place. There always seem to be those few who talk bigger than their boots, make a loud point of showing everybody around them how they're doing their jobs wrong, who go around saying, "This mill can't run without me," when one pair of hands is pretty much as good as another. Joe works a spinwheel of hours that shift week to week, and he fills in on call. He puts in a lot of time and can reel off in his head exactly how many of the 365 days he worked the year before. Usually it's well above 300. On any given day he can also reel off—exactly—how many years and days he has to go until he can retire.

"I'm used to having my own. I've had my own. That don't make me no better than anybody. But I went out there and put my head on the block. I had nine acres of land in 1978."

———

AS THE '90S ENDED, a five-year drought struck, sucking the life out of the Pee Dee. The few small, unirrigated farms that were left just dried out and died.

Joe got out of farming at the turn of the century. The drought didn't do him in; the financing finally caught up to him. He had debt to pay down. The Pee Dee farm was gone. He wasn't getting any younger. The risks just kept piling. He lasted three years doing little more than garden planting, a few rows here and there. Then he began to farm again, less aggressively. What was left of the business already had left him behind. He had to go to a farmer he knew to be schooled.

"Things had changed with chemicals you spray your crops with," he says simply.

Curt McSwain comes from one of the old cotton-gin families in Latta. He sold the business to concentrate on farming. He has that seemingly out-of-kilter country way of holding himself that you find among older farmers in the region. But he stands straight-away to evaluate a stranger with penetrating eyes. He wears a straw hat with a leather band and has a notebook in his shirt pocket with a pencil and a pen. He thinks before he speaks and likes to rest a finger on his temple when he talks. He calls himself a man of traditional values.

"A man is defined by who he stands with or who he has around him," McSwain says with that piercing look in his eyes. Joe has long known and admired McSwain, a successful, large tract farmer. McSwain has no particular reason to help Joe, but he does it because he and Joe share those traditional values.

"It's part of that character thing, work ethic. That draws me," he said. "People who fit in that category need to work together, regardless of cultural differences."

Asked how much farming changed during the few years Joe took his break, McSwain can't help but grin to think about it. "Farming almost exponentially changed," he said. And it continues to change at that pace as soils wear and pests overcome the standard insecticides. Nowadays McSwain is coaching Joe on soybeans because of pest problems with the crop. They talk at the bed of McSwain's truck, and when Joe readies to leave McSwain reminds him simply, "Watch those worms."

———

NEARLY A DECADE after taking that break, Joe eyes the open Pee Dee fields and in his mind still sees them growing. Celeste and he are still trying to pay for the Turner place.

"I'd like to get back into it. I don't want 1,500 acres. I'm fifty-four years old now. I'd like to have some cows, maybe hogs the first go-round. Maybe work about two hundred or three hundred acres. But nothing like I worked in the past. I'd rather farm than do nothing else. But farming just got so expensive."

Celeste gives Joe one of those looks that wives give their husbands—1,500 acres, no way. Not anymore. "He would fall asleep in the truck."

More and more, Joe talks about legacy, all wound up in Scipio's land, talks of leaving something of himself to make his children's lives and their children's lives. Joe has some of Scipio's original land, and that's part of what makes him, he says. You get the sense he sees it as a gift. God had his hands on Scipio, Joe says. His great-great-grandfather had a gift. If you aren't given the gift, you can't catch it. When you are given a gift, you can't mess around; you have to make use of it.

———

ANGELICA IS TWENTY-ONE YEARS OLD, studying chemistry at Clemson University. She was the valedictorian at her high school graduation. She is as lovely as her voice is light, smiles shyly, and is almost sheepish with a visitor. The features of both her parents blend in her features. Her hair is done up and pulled back. She leans forward a little as she talks, her hands folded between her legs as if she were in prayer, the fingers pointed down.

Her dad wanted her to be a dentist. Angelica wants to do pharmaceutical research. Right now, she's researching medical uses of marijuana, a notion that stops Joe short until its commercial value as a pain reliever is explained. A high school science teacher got her interested in chemistry, and she just fell in love with it, she explains. Angelica first drove the 140 Farm Op tractor when she was five and thought it was fun. Nowadays when she comes home for Christmas, she helps her mom in the daycare.

Angelica grew up playing in the yard, following around behind Little Joe, wanting to do what he did, the quintessential younger sibling who wants to be like her older brother. They didn't get to lay around the house: They had to work. Both of them went along with dad from an early age to work the fields. The results were mixed.

"I'd just follow around my dad the whole time. I would just stand there. I didn't do anything. My brother used to get mad because I would always go and just hop in the truck. He would have to stay out in the field, and he would get mad."

Little Joe got mad because Dad would get in the truck to go get something somewhere, and both kids knew that if Joe stopped at the store Angelica would get a cold drink or some other treat.

She's heard little bits of Scipio's story. She is impressed by what he accomplished in that time period, but it's not compelling for her the way it is for Joe. She is aware the land goes back to Scipio, and, in a quiet recognition of that proud old Southern tradition where land makes you who you are, she says it was good of him to get some of his great-grandfather's land. She has a notion of what she would do if she ended up with it.

"I would keep it, because of it being in the family, you know? If I'm in this area I would probably build a house on it." Then she says something remarkable. She wants to build a progressive-care assisted-living home for the elderly. On the land.

———

"LITTLE JOE" Williams is open and direct, a heart as big as his bicep. From early on he rode the tractor sitting up in his dad's lap and got his hands into the motors helping his dad. He has that patient quiet to him of a man who tinkers with machines.

"When we try to get into something on the tractor like the hydraulic hose, so you have to disconnect everything and think it backwards, you try to move as quick as possible and save time, not drag around."

Little Joe has a quiet deference around his father. The two of them understand each other pretty well. "He tried to make sure I went to college and not mess around. When we do he jumps on us," he says.

When Joe goes off on a familiar rant about wanting his children married before they have children but how he'll love his grandchildren no matter what, Little Joe listens intently, stares at the ground between them, his eye with a distant look. Joe will call him "June Bug" to tease him. More often than not, he calls him Junior.

When Joe's driving his little Toyota pickup, he tools about in that slow farmer's crawl that anyone recognizes who's been behind a field truck on a country road the driver calls home. But put Joe behind the wheel of a sedan with a motor under it and he's gone. Little Joe picked that up. He drives a '90s Altima, Nissan's sneaky-fast and surprisingly nimble sports sedan, and he loves to talk cars. Little Joe has that never-met-a-stranger friendliness. "He's a sweet boy. He's got it together," Geraldine says. Women flock to him. Geraldine says he got that from Scipio. He also has that way of listening attentively and then going off and doing his own thing. That, he almost certainly got from Joe.

———

That boy, he's hardheaded. Joe wasn't hardheaded like that. Not like Little Joe. He's bullheaded, I know. That boy that Joe got, he's a good boy. But he would never listen like Joe would listen. When Joe was brought up a grown man, I could tell Joe something, me and Joe would be working at night, planting peas, and you were twenty-something years old, out planting peas and okra.

Geraldine Williams

JOE'S FOOTBALL CAREER might have been ordinary, but there's athleticism in the family. His baby brother, Frank, could put out a 4.2 in the forty-yard dash and had Division 1 college scouts come asking for him. He wasn't any bigger than a bug, but in the '60s a 4.2 was drool stuff even for Div 1. Put a little meat on him and you have a kick returner, maybe a wide receiver. Somebody everybody else was going to have to chase. Joe's daughter and son got some of that. Angelica played basketball all four years at Latta High, while keeping together that valedictorian grade-point average. Little Joe is only 170 pounds, but they're solid. In high school he played outside linebacker/defensive end.

"The hits," he says, is why he played. "I didn't want to get hit, but I like to hit," he says. He shows a thick scar on his arm and pulls up his pants to show a thicker scar on his leg.

"A lot of these cuts are football," he says. He played junior varsity by the seventh grade, and by tenth grade he played some varsity too. By eleventh grade he was varsity and by graduation had people from a local Division 1 school saying, come on out the first year and we'll talk about some scholarship money the second year. Dad kept talking about The Citadel in Charleston, a small school with a good football reputation. The Citadel, though, is a spit-and-polish military school, and the knobs, the freshmen, get the full drill-sergeant treatment of a Marine in basics. They walk around with no hair and that new-guy-in-the-yard look. Dad still brings it up, and Little Joe still gets another kind of look in his eye: Yeah, like that's gonna happen. A small college in Virginia was interested too, but the SATs did him in, and he went to tech school instead, trying to get the grades up.

Little Joe is working twelve-hour night shifts making car tires at Kelly Springfield, in Fayetteville, North Carolina, an hour or so up the road from Latta. Asked what he would do with his dad's land, he gets thoughtful.

"I'd keep it. Just 'cause of the history, passed down from my dad to me. I could pass it on to my kids. I'd do something with it. Farm it. Plant it. Garden on it."

Right now, Little Joe is trying to pass the certification test to become a mortician. He's missed twice, the last time by a hair. Joe asks if he is studying, and he says, a little. Don't mess around, Joe tells him.

"I've got to look out for Little Joe right now. Angelica has the best business head right now. Little Joe don't have the best business head right now. His best business head is girls, chasing a frock tail. That's his business. A frock tail. Chasing a frock tail. That's Little Joe's dream, right now."

———

JOE WAS STRICT with his kids growing up, prodded them relentlessly to get their education, an echo of his own raising. Kirby, the Latta schools superintendent, will tell you that in all his forty-one years in the schools, Joe stands as one of the top ten parents with the highest expectations for his children. Joe is straight-at-you and relentless even describing it.

"My philosophy about life, you've got a problem, you adjust it then. You bend that sapling while it's small. You don't wait until it gets fifteen years old and try to adjust it. You adjust them then. You try to raise a child, you tell them something, you mean it. When they do wrong, if you let them get away with it, you can't hold on to this.

"I told both my kids, you go to school, you get an education. If somebody jumps on you, and you can't get around it, go to a teacher or whatever, you got to fight, you got to fight. Don't let nobody hurt you. That's what you've got to do. I told the teachers every year, and I tell them, if there's a problem with 'em you can't handle, why don't y'all call me, and I promise you I'll be there. And I told my daughter the same thing."

When Angelica rented an apartment at college, Celeste and Joe drove across the state with her to have a look. Joe put together the bed for her, lecturing the whole time about how she has an opportunity. She is there to get an education, and that's what she should be doing. This bed is for you, he told her, not for a boy. He'll come back up if she needs him, if she's sick or something. It better not be to fix a mess. When he was her age, he was working in the fields, he says. In fact, he was working in the fields a lot younger than that.

"My momma had seven kids before she ever married. I was the oldest boy," Joe says. "Now my kids helped me when I was farming. But they never had to stay out of school to help me. I made sure they went to school and got an education. The Lord blessed me that I was able to do that. Now, my momma, she done the best she could. She done the best that she could. Back in those days, there weren't no kind of help for a lady that got four, five, seven kids, back in those days."

When Joe wants to make a point, his voice gets loud, strident. The words come like a finger prodding.

"My kid, she knows right now. I get up and talk to them, she don't throw cunning on me. She knows not to say no to Joe Williams. She knows that. I love my young'uns. I tell them. Both my young'uns know right now. I ain't gonna put my hands on them and go wild when they go wrong. But they know. They do right by me. I'm not going to put up with this foolishness."

———

JOE NEVER STRUCK Little Joe. When they acted up as kids, mom got the switch. A lot of times it was because Joe wasn't there. Not always. He took a belt to Angelica—one time, when she was a young teen—for showing some sass. He cringes a little to talk about it.

Chapter 12

Home

WHEN YOU COME into South Carolina from North Carolina along I-95, the land drops off below the road grade, and you get the first real feel of what will become the lowcountry, the sense that this place gets swamped.

It's the Little and then the Big Pee Dee, the first prominent natural signs that you are someplace different. The planter country of Latta essentially rests in the arms of the two rivers. The official name for the Big Pee Dee is the Great Pee Dee River, but nobody calls it that.

The Little Pee Dee is one of those almost surreal blackwater passages, the kind of stream where civilization can disappear for miles at a time and you are lost in a meander of sand bars, huge bole cypress, wild azalea, and spider lilies. It's a seemingly primeval place of exotic creatures, heron, ibises, swallowtailed kites, secluded bends where wood duck startle like ghosts and hag fish rise like longnose gar and then, farther down, the mother of them all, the American alligator, whose nearly submerged eyes bead up at boaters from the water surface and whose inhuman size can make you catch your breath.

Maybe the wildest way to think of the Little Pee Dee is yazoos. Yazoos are streams that would be tributaries of the river if they could reach it. Because the river is plowing its way through the coastal floodplain through its huge sand-dune deposits and the like, all the while dumping silt, the river creates natural levees. Streams that would feed into it hit those levees and turn, running along-side the river a way until there's a breach. Sometimes they run in the river's own abandoned streambeds. Like the river itself, the yazoos leave oxbow lakes, guts, and backswamps. That's the Little Pee Dee, a slew of backswamps.

The Big Pee Dee is a *river*, a brawly, swirling mass of water and wetlands that can flood a basin a mile or more wide before anybody begins to worry about it. There's a tragic story that says a lot about just how vast and thick are the bottoms of this river basin. In 2004 a U.S. Army Black Hawk helicopter crashed in the woods, just off I-95. Three soldiers in the flight crew died. The copter is one those behemoth craft used at times to transport troops; it's not the sort of thing that could slip out of the sky and not leave a mark. It was one of two helicopters flying on a routine training mission from Fort Bragg, North Carolina, to Florence, just a few miles down the road from the river. The weather was bad, and something went wrong. Searchers knew about where the crash had happened; the other copter had been in contact. But an air search covered 120 square miles without a sign, and after twenty-four hours of searches nobody could say where the big Black Hawk and its crew had ended up. Then an over-the-road truck driver on I-95 happened to glance at the right spot while crossing the river and spotted the wreckage along the bank.

———

CONSERVATION GROUPS in North Carolina like to call the Pee Dee basin the cradle of civilization in the Carolinas. That's a little much. But this is a river system that starts as a mountain creek in the Blue Ridge and passes through country where there's literally gold in them thar hills. A twelve-year-old boy living in the Uwharrie Mountains in 1799 was scrambling along a creek when he came across a cool-looking, seventeen-pound yellow rock. The family put it to good use for a few years as a doorstop, until somebody stumbled over it who knew better. His mouth dropped open, and a gold rush ensued.

By the time the Pee Dee reaches South Carolina, the gold has turned to sand, and nowadays the river has already been dammed and released a half dozen times or more.

———

THERE'S A TANGENTIAL but pretty funny story about the state line with North Carolina. It was supposed to be a straight line along the thirty-fifth parallel, starting from a point not far from the Big Pee Dee and only about thirty miles northwest of Joe's house. From there the line was to run west to the Chattooga River, where in 1813 surveyors etched their mark into a streambound boulder that became known as Commissioner's Rock. Except the line didn't. The surveyors made their way northwest from Little River to the parallel line, trundling through so much marsh, muck and stickerbushes that they didn't make very good time even getting there and season to season were forced to mark their progress leaving blazes on trees and on other not-so-sure spots to find their way back.

Then they weren't quite sure exactly where the parallel was. Part of the problem, according to legend, was the proximity of a corn-liquor still. Laugh that off if you want, but a 1905 survey apparently adjusted the line through Marlboro County to accommodate a few stills and bars that wanted to operate—legally—out of South Carolina. The new line was drawn finely enough that the customers of one bar could sit in North Carolina and lean forward to drink in South Carolina.

Anyhow, the 1813 surveyors missed. The line was drawn starting some twelve miles south of where it should have been. The legend says that after a night at the still, the surveyors staggered to their feet and simply started west from where they were. The two states have fussed over the line ever since. Among the disputes is just which state President Andrew Jackson was born in.

The punch line to the story isn't so funny. In the 1990s, the Carolinas agreed to the Joint Boundary Commission—yet one more pounding of the stakes to try to get the thing right. In 2011 the commission was still tweaking a new line through stores and subdivision homes—displacing people who bought, built, or went into business specifically wanting one state's set of rules or taxes only to find out they have to live with another. The new line between Mecklenburg County in North Carolina and Lancaster County in South Carolina ran through six homes in three consecutive cul de sacs in one subdivision alone, according to commission documents. It ran across one homeowner's patio.

———

ROCKED BY SURVEYORS OR NOT, the Pee Dee "cradle" has been home to people for a long time. The rivers were named for the native Americans who lived in communities along them and for whom the streams were the highways and the farm for foods like chestnuts, strawberries, plums, corn, and beans. The word "Pee Dee" is thought to be a corruption of one of two Catawba words, *pi ri,* meaning something that's good, or *pi here,* meaning capable.

The Pee Dees, like most of the other native coastal communities, are waging a dug-in siege to be recognized as a tribe. It's one of those Catch-22 pursuits where you have to convince the government you really do exist, that you haven't been wiped out. The coastal tribes go at it doggedly, for pride, sure, but for a lot more. These are peoples who for generations didn't talk about who they were, because the discrimination was even worse than African Americans saw.

Against the jihad that was colonial white coastal settlement, the few survivors of various tribal communities banded together, so tribal lines were blurred. They intermarried with blacks, Hispanics, and whites, so racial lines were blurred. So the tribes today aren't any more than remnants. Their documented histories are English scraps and asides in journals of Spanish explorers. Try sorting out all that and footnoting it in a legal document to present to the South Carolina Indian Affairs Commission.

And the door prize is just as elusive—federal status, that golden coin jingling into the cash-spewing slot machine of casino-financed sovereignty. The feds don't like to just give away people or sovereignty, so some tribes have been seeking the status for more than a century. State status, which the Pee Dee won in 2006, is the first legal bar to hurdle and carries perks like permission to sell crafts and trinkets as authentic tribal goods.

So, trinkets are most of what's left of the native heritage in a region where state archaeologists in the late 1990s brushed dirt off a notched stone spear point that dated to the melting of the last Ice Age, unearthed a five-thousand-year-old patterned pottery shard made using Spanish moss. Nearby were a petrified chunk of tree that looked like a brick, the craftworked rim of an 1830s pottery cup, and the shank of an eighteenth-century tobacco pipe with the initials "T.D."

Those finds were made at the Kolb site near Mechanicsville, on a bluff over an oxbow lake that was once the bank of the Great Pee Dee River. The bank, it turns out, has been camped on by virtually every prehistoric and historic people known to have lived in the region.

It's about ten miles from Joe's home.

———

THE PEE DEE is a changeable beast. Despite the river's belt-loosening girth, it nearly ran dry in the five-year drought at the turn of the twenty-first century. The situation got so bad that at one point saltwater backed up fifteen miles from the river's ocean mouth, shutting down a Georgetown fresh-drinking-water intake. The crisis spurred the state to challenge North Carolina in a Supreme Court "water wars" lawsuit over just how much of the flow the Tar Heel state could hold back in its upstream lakes. The two states eventually settled the suit, with little change except for a provision that North Carolina has to tell South Carolina if it pulls water from one river basin and deposits it in another, the sort of thing that wouldn't take long to be made public anyhow with the profusion of riverkeepers and other environmental groups keeping an eye out. In fact, the lawsuit was filed in the wake of an environmentalist's alert that just such an "interbasin transfer" was taking place along the Catawba River. The settlement between the states also includes a provision that either side can sue in the future.

There's another quirky little footnote to this river. Along its lower stretch near Georgetown, if you slog through the muddy cypress bottom of Carver's Bay, you come across something that looks, in the words of one observer, like an old horse trough. Water is being carried in a concrete flume literally over the top of the wetlands.

The flume is part of a zigzagging canal built in the 1950s, during another severe drought, to ensure that the town's International Paper plant had a supply of fresh water. A civil engineer studying a topo map realized that he could supply the plant with a gravity feed of fresh water from a ridge along a bend in the river farther upstream by running the flume along the ridge line for twenty-seven miles all the way down to the plant. A gravity feed. More or less. The canal needed two of those flumes and two sets of pumps—one to lift water from the Pee Dee and the second to lift it back up after the canal tunnels under the Black River.

But the contraption works, so matter-of-factly that for a while after the flow started, people took to riding pickup trucks down the road alongside it, towing water skiers and shooting doves as they went. In 2010, the canal was still supplying fresh water to both the plant and the city. It's so distinct that you can see it if you Google up a satellite image of the region.

———

FEWER THAN TEN MILES east of Latta, the Little Pee Dee crosses the line between Dillon and Marion Counties at Buck Swamp, a name that says it all if you're a deer hunter. Among the swamp's first settlers was John Bethea III, the man who built that 1798 cotton press now sitting on the road into Latta. His nickname was "Buckswamp."

———

THE TWO STREAMS are the heart of the place, but, oddly enough, Joe has had little to do with either one, other than tilling the soils. The Big Pee Dee is just something to look at. Jimmy Moody explains that while the Little Pee Dee is blackwater, the Big Pee Dee is brown water, a muddy river. Copeland Moody took his children swimming in the Little Pee Dee at Floydale Bridge landing when they were younger, as a reward for doing chores. The family had quit that by the time Joe showed up.

Joe's tie to the rivers is in his ways, the ways of the Pee Dee country, as seasoned and winding as the streams themselves. The rivers and bottoms are your life. The most prosperous-looking store in Latta is an outdoorsman shop with camouflage hunting outfits on mannequins in the window. You're as likely to see a fishing pole as a gun racked up in a pickup. It's nothing to drive across a two-lane backroad bridge and wave to a solitary old man or woman who waves back at you while dangling a pole over a swamp, just to pass the time and maybe hook a dinner of bowfin.

Joe doesn't fish. He can remember only a time or two, when he was younger, at a farm pond. He doesn't hunt, something a little unusual for anybody who lives in the Carolinas country, where you can put up in the freezer a winter's worth of venison. Asked about it, he hesitates a moment, then says he just never had the time. No, he shakes his head, he's never gone down to the river much. But when he crosses one of the Pee Dees, he takes a moment to glimpse the breast of the river flow. He knows he's home.

———

Joe will call Copeland Moody "Mr. Copeland," but sometimes almost stops himself doing it. Times have changed. He met up with Moody after he died, in the yard behind the old house, back by the trailer. One evening he went out in the backyard to a storage trailer and Moody sat there under the live oak trees by the grill, just like he used to.

Moody said, "How you doin', Boy?" Joe said he was doing well. Moody said, "Heard you were getting married." Joe said he was and asked Moody what he thought of Celeste.

"She's a good girl," Moody said. Then he disappeared.

The night Celeste and Joe brought Little Joe home from the hospital, they set him up just outside the bedroom door, because the crib wouldn't fit inside. Late in the night Joe was startled awake.

"The crib started shaking. And I jumped up and put the light on and the crib was just laying right there. It didn't wake him up or nothing. It was a curious feeling, you know what I mean? I was like, what's that?"

Afterward, when Joe mentioned the oddity to an older person, he was asked if the owner who built the home had died. A shaking crib is a sign the owner came and gave the infant a gift, a talent. That's what they always used to say.

Irene Moody has come back, too, more recently, when Joe was asleep in his bed.

"She tried to tell me something, Mrs. Moody did. I don't know what. I waked up out of the bed and she come and stood over me and she wanted, she said, she was trying to tell me something. I don't know what."

Scipio Williams has not appeared, but he seems to be around.

"Every time I'm on Grandpa's farm I feel something for him. I feel like he's right there. We didn't get the whole four hundred acres back. But that fifty acres we got it, that means more to me than if I had a million dollars. That's what we originated from."

Chapter 13

The House with Slaves

THE ROAD OUT OF LATTA that goes past the high school turns into a country two-lane rumpling by the trim white stones of the city cemetery. A turn to the left beyond the ornate stones goes down to the centuries-old Okra Point Cemetery, the black graveyard, where crumbling and overgrown headstones straggle into the hillside and pines shoot up among them. Cracked hardwood and live oak are hung with moss. The mood is a funereal neglect. The dates and the stones get older, worn, and harder to read as you work your way back and gradually fall away into the woods and weeds. It's a good idea to keep an eye to the ground as you walk, to watch out for copperheads. Somewhere in there they say Scipio Williams is buried. Or maybe not.

On the other side of Temperance Hill is the tiny town of Sellers, where the sole store is the Williams Grocery, a place everybody calls the Sellers store. Down the way from the store and over the rail tracks is Slabtown Road, one of those country two-lanes that rambles back through farm fields, bottoms, and pine stands. A lot of the homes have that ramshackle look, board cabins built-as-you-go. Back in one of those pine stands is the old Red Hill Cemetery, and back among those plots some of the Williamses are said to be buried. Frank Jones, former mayor of Sellers and a former lieutenant on its police force, leads Joe into the undergrowth on a warm January day.

Jones knows the graveyard well enough to remember seeing the name Williams, but he shakes his head at the name Scipio Williams. That one he doesn't remember. He talks about the last time he was back there in the '70s, hunting a murder suspect. Joe remembers the case, and they go back and forth about the details as they step over and around tree-limb debris and thorn bushes. A woman who lives nearby and who went to high school with Joe has warned them to watch for her hogs, which she just let loose back there. The ground is leaf covered and the day is warm enough that you keep an eye out for snakes here, too, even though they aren't likely to be too interested if they are out.

The suspect, it turns out, wasn't ever captured. After a week or so in the woods, he turned himself in to his employer, who took him down to the jail. Enough was enough.

For no apparent reason, Jones stops and says, "There it is." Over to his left, sticking out of tangles of pine needles and leaves, are a few old headstones. On a closer look, the ground is pocked with the ghost holes of sunken grave sites. Most of them no longer have a headstone, if they once did. The men pick their way from stone to stone: White, Miles, the inscriptions read, White, Miles. One of the oldest-looking stones sits all but by itself in the shade of a straggle of small trees. The stone has those green and brown age stains from moss, lichen, or just soil and rain. The inscription stops you cold: Laura M., wife of S.W. Williams. The tombstone next to her is a White. There's no sign of another stone or tomb nearby, much less a relatively sizeable one like you'd expect for Scipio Williams.

The inscription says she was born in 1847, which dovetails with the understanding that Laura was younger than Scipio, who was born in 1836. She died in 1901, preceding Scipio, which is a given since the estate was divided among the children and guardianship was an issue. The "M" is a puzzle if she was a Crawford, though it doesn't surprise Jones to find it on the tombstone. The Mileses, he recalls, were kin to the Williamses.

But, one way or another, there's no Scipio Williams headstone to be found. Despite Laura's apparent gravesite and the cemetery stories, it's hard to shake the notion that Scipio could very well have been buried on his own land. Joe hasn't found any sign of that on his acres. The owners of the larger parcel, who sold him his acres, never spoke of it. There's no mention in the Letters Testamentary.

Wherever Scipio is laid has been lost to time. The Sellers cemetery, oddly enough, is just down the road from the Pee Dee lands Joe worked for years.

JOE WANTS TO OPEN a funeral home with Little Joe, right where Scipio's old house stood. Scipio built coffins.

"And I wonder, did he build his own? Did he build his own coffin?" Joe asks. "We plan to build, when we get straightened out, the funeral home right by Scipio's house. It's just a coincidence, you know, the fact that a great-great-grandson would come along and build a funeral home where he used to build a coffin. It's strange, you know what I mean? It's very strange. And I would name the chapel after him anyhow."

The funeral home is an odd preoccupation for Joe, one that's been with him most of his life. In small towns, funeral directors tend to be relatively prosperous, something that wouldn't be lost on a country kid living in a tenant shack. But there's more to it than that.

On a hot summer afternoon, settled back on his mother's porch with a visitation taking place down the street and the deceased a person of some size, Joe starts talking about the difficulty of handling some bodies. Geraldine isn't particularly enthused. But on a country porch, talk is entertainment and nobody's going anywhere.

"You can take antifreeze, mix with that embalming fluid, and bring that swelling down," Joe says.

"Mmhm," Geraldine says.

"You can take shoe polish and do a miracle with it, on a dark-complexioned person or brown."

Joe talks about seeing a body at a viewing and the stitches showing where they put his head back on after the autopsy. He wanted to tell them all they needed to do was get PVC pipe to prop up the decapitated head or broken neck, literally glue it on, then hide the tear with makeup.

"Samuel Jackson was the best embalmer we ever had in Latta. He could make a face. He could make them pretty," Geraldine says.

Joe gets almost reverent talking about caring for the bodies. He began helping out at a funeral home in his late twenties. Just took to it, he says, something he can't really explain. Part of the appeal, for sure, was just the mechanics of it. Part of it was something more. For sure there is the memory of Copeland Moody. Joe was still a young teen when he tended to Copeland as he passed, death rattle and all. But Joe says no, it's something deeper than that. He remembers as a child he would ride with Geraldine to funerals.

———

IN THE RURAL SOUTH, as much as or more than anywhere else, funerals are social tradition. People put on their finery. Meals are served. Any number of customs attend the rites, including, in the lowcountry, holdovers from Gullah culture: If a new mother dies, the baby is passed over the casket to keep the mother's spirit from haunting the child. Gullah funeralgoers tend to wear white rather than dark colors. White is considered the color of high mourning, a sign of the eternal.

The traditions of the rice-growing peoples were so strong that, as communities moved inland after the Civil War, they tried to bring rice growing with them, as far upstream as the swamping lowcountry would allow them. But rice didn't grow well inland, and they moved to other crops. In the same way, the oral traditions and social customs have morphed with the times, lost and taken on nuances.

Gullah itself is a product of nuances. Almost arbitrarily, the Gullah Geechee West African culture has been delineated a rice-growing sea-island tradition of South Carolina, Georgia, and Florida, Gullah identified largely with South Carolina and Geechee with Georgia and Florida. The traditions are a weave as fine and as functional as a sweetgrass basket—ways of craftsmanship, cooking, singing, and the like—that kept West African customs alive among relatively isolated slaves left largely on their own on the remote islands. The culture's most remarkable feature might be its defining one: Gullah is a pattern of language, almost a patois. Marquetta Goodwine of St. Helena Island is the internationally recognized Queen Quet, founder of the Gullah/Geechee Sea Island Coalition. Queen Quet describes Gullah as a language of African words, phonetic structure, and syntax, while Geechee is a dialect bridging Gullah and English, borrowing English words and using Gullah structure and syntax. Gullah words have been woven into the language of the lowcountry today, words like "benne" for sesame. You may have heard of benne wafers.

There's two points to be made in this. First of all, the words "Gullah" and "Geechee" themselves are of nebulous origins and have taken on new meanings. Gullah is sometimes said to be a corruption of Angola, one of those West African nations and the home country of many of the earliest slaves. But the words also are said to echo the names of West African peoples, such as Gola, Kissi, Mende, Temne, Twi, and Vai, as the *New Georgia Encyclopedia* points out.

And it wasn't just sea-island slaves that came from rice-growing West African cultures. Virginia slaves such as Scipio's father did too. Except they ended up growing tobacco and worked closer with whites—side by side, at least in the early days: less isolation, less hold on the traditions.

———

IN JOE'S COMMUNITY, there's no baby-passing coffin custom, but there is a tradition of wearing white. And there is The Step. The lead pallbearer coming out of the church with the coffin will carry it in a military-style march as a sign of respect.

"They lean back on the casket and they come out with that step, like Michael Jackson doing the moon walk," Joe says.

Because a funeral carries the social import of a formal party, individual funeralgoers also pick up their own customs and carry them out almost superstitiously funeral to funeral. Geraldine has a custom of touching the cheek of the deceased and then kissing it.

"Some people say it's nasty," she says with a shrug in her voice. For her, it's a carryover from the death of her baby, John F. Kennedy Williams, in 1963, from a bleeding ulcer when he was only five months old.

"My baby died in my arms. I kissed that baby. I kissed that baby. I thought it would help," she said. "I never thought I'd get over that."

———

FUNERALS LEAVE their imprint on a kid, and the first time tends to haunt: The pasty body is disorienting and scary, and the cries or hushed tones of the mourners' voices reinforce that. The people who run funerals, with their dark formal clothes and somber faces, have that air of dominion. For a kid coming in from the fields, where even a passing car was something to watch, the experience was indelible.

"I don't know if some of that rubbed off then," Joe says. "Grandpa, he built coffins."

———

JOE'S REVERENCE for the bodies and his craftsman's interest in the mechanics of handling them made him a pretty unusual young man coming into his own in the 1970s. He went funeral home to funeral home looking for "an opportunity to get behind the walls." But with no real background or training, he could get only a few chances to help out front. Until he ran into Sam Bartell. The owner of Bartell's Funeral Home was a quiet man with a steadying manner and keen insight.

"If he could help someone he would," says Flossie Bartell, his wife. "That's why the business is. He died, and there were people who owed him. But he didn't worry about that. His attitude was, when it comes in it will pay the bills."

Bartell married the younger Flossie Bartell, when she was twenty-five years old. He took in her three children and told Flossie not to bother going to court for child support—if the father wasn't man enough to raise them, he would. She had a GED and a good-paying job at a pharmaceutical plant. Bartell saw she had a lot more. He prodded her to go back to school and took over the day-to-day minding of the kids while she did and while he worked. She went on to get a doctorate and make a career in education. Even when she was earning more money than he was, Bartell paid bills like her car tax and insurance, telling her it was his responsibility.

He invested all his profits back into the funeral home. She didn't get that for a long time, she says. Then her older husband began nudging her to get a funeral director's license. When Bartell got sick, she took over, and since he died the business has taken care of her.

———

WHEN JOE AND BARTELL MET, these were two people who recognized each other. Oddly enough, they even resembled each other. Bartell put him right to it, helping staff a funeral. By the early '90s, Joe was behind the wall, back in the embalming room. It wasn't long before Bartell told him, "You've got a lifetime contract with me, son." From the time they met, Sam would talk to Flossie about Joe Williams. Like Joe, Bartell had picked up an interest in mortuary work at a young age and it stuck. As a child, he wanted to be a policeman, Flossie Bartell says, but a cousin he looked up to, who was a policeman in New York, was killed in the line of duty. By the time Bartell graduated from high school, he had decided he wanted to go to morticians' school.

Nobody took it seriously, except Sam Bartell. He graduated morticians' school at twenty years old, so quickly he was a year too young to get his license. So he took an uncertified laborer's job in a funeral home until he could get the certification.

As for Joe, "I think he liked the fact that Joe had a vision. He had a plan. I for one believe it's going to materialize, because if you can dream it you can do it," Flossie Bartell says. A lot like Sam Bartell, Joe is one of those singular men with determination, drive. If he puts his mind to something, he's going to get it done. She and Sam talked about it all the time.

"If you could take that and give it to your children they would be all right, you think, with their youth and all the doors that are open that they could go through."

———

An embalming is one of those you-don't-want-to-be-there experiences. How it goes, Joe tells you, will rock your mind.

The first time Flossie Bartell saw one, she had inadvertently walked in on her husband working on a body that had undergone a complete autopsy. After a complete autopsy, a funeral home doesn't get the body; it gets the pieces. The job is to put them back together.

"I won't tell you what I saw. It didn't bother me in that I was afraid or anything, but it was just something I didn't care to see," she said. To this day, while running a funeral home, she goes back to the embalming room only to do the hair of a female deceased—after everything else has been taken care of.

Little Joe's first body unnerved him. It was a big elderly woman in dreadlocks, and he had to help wash and massage her; when rigor has set in, the muscles get massaged to help loosen them back to a lifelike shape. A few of the other students had to sew the head back on. One time he had to sew a stomach back together. The first few bodies you work hesitantly, half-convinced they are going to wake up, Little Joe says. It takes a while for the cold reality to set in.

Joe's first time, "It was pitiful. It makes you think." What sticks with him most about it—watching the cutting and knowing the body felt no pain. That will be you one day, he thought.

To handle an embalming, you have to love the work, Joe says. You have to love it. He talks about it almost spiritually, and for sure the procedure has that sacrificial aura to it. But the job is part blood technician, part make-up artist. An embalming table has the weirdly disconcerting feel of an operating table or an examination table in a doctor's office. A nearby counter or shelf is stacked with rows of plastic containers that look like liter milk cartons. The liquids in the containers are a palette of colors, like selections of sports drinks. Embalming fluid, as it turns out, isn't any one fluid; it's a variety. The colors are dyes used to simulate as much of "natural" flesh tones as possible. Different fluids perform different functions: Some of them puff up a sunken-in corpse to make it look more alive; some of them take the bloat out of a swollen body.

The corpse, if it's in any condition to, gets a slit cut into an artery or vein right at the breastbone and a pump hose inserted. A second slit is cut wherever feasible, places like the jugular, the wrist, or even the heart. That's where the blood runs out, down along a channel at the rim of the table. Aneurysm hooks are placed into each slit to keep clots from plugging up the works. Sometimes multiple incisions have to be made to get all the blood out.

The pump is calibrated to push hard enough to make the fluids flow, but not any harder; the flow has to be watched so you don't end up bloating the body with embalming fluid. It's designed, in other words, to pump at just about the speed of a human heart.

The fun starts once everything is drained and the body filled with a few liters full of colorized preservative. Loose ends get sewed on, PVC or whatever set in place to prop up everything so the body looks "at rest" in the coffin. The jaws are pried apart to keep the mouth from having that sucked-in look. Putty is placed in the mouth to fill out the jaws. There are little tricks like eye caps to make sure the closed eyes still have that globe shape and to make sure they stay shut.

Nothing disrupts the solemnity of a viewing like the corpse opening an eye for glimpse. The restored face gets its rouges, blush, and powders just as a woman would make herself up in front of a mirror for a night out. It is, in fact, the last night out for most corpses.

————

WITH ALL THE OTHER parallels in Joe's life, it's almost too much that the social tradition of embalming in the United States started with Abraham Lincoln and the Civil War.

The art of preserving bodies had been performed for ages, everything from mummifying to leaving bodies frozen in a shed until they could be buried after the spring thaw. The use of chemicals to keep a body from stinking was just beginning to catch on in Europe when the war broke out, as John Cooney tells it in *Obit Magazine* (yes, there really is an *Obit Magazine*). Little more than a month into the fighting, Colonel Elmer Ellsworth bravely tried to pull a Confederate flag from the roof of the Marshall House Hotel in Alexandria, Virginia. Somebody took exception and shot Ellsworth dead.

Ellsworth, a lawyer, had clerked for Lincoln in Lincoln's Springfield, Illinois, practice back in the pre-presidential days. The two had been good friends. Lincoln asked that the body be brought to the White House to lie in state. That required keeping it fresh for a time. Thomas Holmes, a New York doctor and coroner, had been messing with a French preserving technique and offered to do the job. Mary Lincoln made what became the classic funeral-cliché comment that the colonel looked like he was sleeping—and the embalming business was off and running.

It wasn't too long before the massive slaughter made it big business. The fields were so plied with bodies that burying them before they stank too badly became a logistical nightmare, the task of identifying each one too overwhelming. The folks back home were appalled. Thousands of slaves trailed along behind Confederate general Robert E. Lee's army, each picking his way through the horror to find his master's body. Relatives began turning out on battlefields to bring home their own, using meager, melting supplies of ice to preserve the remains. That did the job so poorly that railroads refused to transport them, Cooney writes.

So Lincoln ordered that Union soldiers be embalmed—launching a profitable if grotesque cottage industry. Holmes himself made a fortune on it, embalming more than four thousand bodies at $100 apiece. He sold his homebrew fluid of arsenic, alcohol, chlorides, creosote, mercuric chlorides, turpentine, and zinc for $3 a gallon to other "embalmer-surgeons," Cooney notes. Those guys made their way through camps before battle to get payment in advance of $25 for soldiers and $50 for officers, and before long they upped the fees to $30 and $80. That didn't do much for morale, so the military stepped in, banning the tent flap-to-tent flap sales. The businesses moved to shops set up in tents alongside the camps, where the "embalmer-surgeons" insisted that officers' bodies be sent: Officers were more likely to have people back home who could afford to pay for the preservation and shipping. It was in essence the birth of the modern funeral business.

Poignantly, within a year of Ellsworth's death, Lincoln would have his son, Todd, embalmed after losing him to typhoid fever, Cooney notes. Three years later, Mary Lincoln would have Lincoln embalmed.

JOE WANTED to go to embalming school in Georgia, he says. But then he met Celeste—"When you went and got that woman," his mom kids him with a sharp laugh—so the notion got sidetracked for a while. But in 1996, he had just come out of bankruptcy when a man came to him needing investors for a funeral home the man wanted to build in a town nearby. Joe wanted in. It nudged that already prodding notion in the back of his mind and had the appeal of a good investment. He told himself it would be a good learning process, a chance to get his feet wet, so to speak.

"Sometimes when you're young you get an ambition," he says. "You don't study things out." He chipped in with three other people. One of them was a troubled soul, Joe says succinctly. The partnership immediately got off on the wrong foot, naturally over just what had happened to the investment money. Joe describes the ordeal as a mess and a roller-coaster ride. But, if anything, the experience made him more serious about opening his own home. Besides, one day Little Joe came to him. He decided to be a mortician.

"I said, 'Son, I ain't going to tell you that that don't make me happy. But Joe, I don't want you to go, not on account of me. I want you to go because you want to go.'"

THE BUSINESS WILL BE the Williams Funeral Home, Joe says. He's talking branches. He has scouted communities for locations and settled on three. He wants to be secure when it's all said and done, he says. The chapel will be called

Joe Williams in back of his home and the shed where he lived as a young teen in the 1960s.
Courtesy of Benton Henry Photography.

the Scipio Williams Memorial Chapel. The first one he thought about putting on Scipio's land, talked about it as a Williams tradition, a legacy.

"I'm hoping the children take it and grow with it. My granddaddy Scipio Williams, right out on that place, built coffins for the old funeral homes. Now he's got a great-great-great-grandson who is a mortician. I'm hoping one day to build a funeral home right out on that site. And it's a strange thing how that stuff will work out, isn't it?"

But business will be business, and for a while now Joe also has had his eye on an old white manor house in downtown Latta, one of those chambered homes with solemn wood floors, that feels like a chapel the moment you step through the foyer. You could set up an embalming room in the kitchen that opens to a long porch out back, put up a ramp, and roll the caskets back and forth from the hearse. On the far end of the 4,500-square-foot manor is a cloistered study with a fireplace. This, Joe thinks, could be the Scipio Williams Chapel.

The house is a turn-of-the-twentieth-century farmhouse, not all that dissimilar from Scipio's peg-and-stile house. There's another oddity about it that appeals to Joe: a collection of grayed clapboard structures out back that include of tobacco bulk barn and smokehouse. They look for the world like old slave cabins.

———

Other than the funeral home, Joe's doing everything he said he was going to do, and he's been doing that all his life.

Jimmy Moody

Chapter 14

An Aroma like Sweet Grass

IN LATTA'S OWN little history book, a typed manuscript subtitled "Home of Champions," author Christopher Lynn Bethea writes with the folk touch that a lot of people in small rural places have. He calls the town's first high school "the old red brick building," the way older folks in Latta like to remember it. He defines times in terms of disasters, talking about the year the old red brick building burned.

For generations, Latta was one of those classic Southern stopping-in towns along the rail line and then one of the major roads that carried Northerners back and forth to Florida vacations. The roads back then tended to follow the rails. The towns each grew a collection of main-strip businesses that catered to those travelers, a sort of hometown Stuckey's row. People who were raised in St. George, farther south in the state along the same route, would later remember having to wait for minutes at a time to cross the road during season. The notion became almost surreal after I-95 was built a little farther to the west and, one by one, the motels and souvenir shops and even the restaurants closed down. Thirty years later their shells still stand, crumpling or crumbled, straggled with kudzu and ruin. You could sunbathe on the empty roads and the few local motorists would know enough to drive around you.

———

PLANS CALL FOR I-73 to run right through Temperance Hill. The interstate is conceived as a $2 billion, ninety-mile-long span from the North Carolina sand-hills to the glitter speckle of touristy Myrtle Beach, right down the flank of the Cape Fear Arch. It's the last leg of a longer interstate highway, and it's derided as the Ohio Highway to the beach.

You have to understand Myrtle Beach to understand what this is all about. The place is the carnival stuffed-animal prize of the Southeast coast. It's the only beach town in South Carolina where there's one of those Million Dollar Miles of high-rise beach hotels forming a huge wall along the Atlantic. They just finished a fancy boardwalk, and entrepreneurs have built a huge Ferris wheel right there on the beach. It's no coincidence that Little River, a few miles to the north, became one of the first casino-boat destinations in a state where gambling is the sort of evil decried from the pulpit on Sunday.

Myrtle is iconic. When people who live in the North Carolina Piedmont some two hundred miles west say "the Beach," they're headed for Myrtle. Anywhere else and they'll name the beach, just so there isn't confusion. When Joe was asked to describe how it felt to buy that first piece of Scipio's old land, he said it was like buying a piece of downtown Myrtle Beach. His family doesn't vacation often, but when they do they go to Myrtle. The place advertises itself as the only beach town with one hundred golf courses. One hundred courses. Myrtle is the T-shirt everybody wants to bring home and the ATM of what's said to be a $16 billion tourism industry in the state.

On top of that, a bee swarm of sunseekers and retirees converged on the place in the 1990s, turning it into one of the fastest-growing areas in the country. Subdivisions now cul-de-sac their way back into the pocosin pines, swamplands so thick with peat bogs, pine needles, and assorted accelerants that lightning-strike wildfires naturally groomed the old longleaf savannahs that used to dominate the landscape—fires so prevalent they came to serve a vital role in the ecosystem. Then the land became timber plantation, loblolly and slash pine. A forestry gauge of natural flammable material estimates there's now fifteen to twenty tons of it per acre in those pines. That's fuel for the sort of catastrophic fires seen in arid Western states. The largest blaze in South Carolina's history scorched thirty thousand acres of the pocosin back in the 1970s, in the timber plantation days.

Nowadays, you have piles and piles of subdivisions dumped right on top of the pocosin. A fire in 2009 scorched thirty square miles, destroyed or damaged more than 150 homes. It's a revealing aside that a month after that massive April blaze, beetles came out like a plague to finish off the burned pine trees. They were stopped by a profusion of the very rare Venus fly trap—that creepy, spiky bug eater you don't find anywhere else in the world. Fly traps popped up in long swaths through the charred pines, thousands on thousands. Even biologists who know how resilient the ecosystem is and how vital fire is to it were astonished. Most years you could prowl through the prickly undergrowth for an acre and be lucky to find a fly trap. They had never seen anything like that.

Welcome to the beach, folks.

And folks, of course, are still coming. Myrtle Beach was one of a handful of areas in the country where housing construction didn't ground to a complete halt during the 2008 recession.

———

ROADHOUSES are the nightlife in country church communities, late-hour taverns that proprietors call private clubs to skirt local liquor laws. They're usually not much more than cinder-block buildings with a handpainted or spray-painted sign on the wall. They are infamous among sheriffs' deputies for drugs and late-night shootings. Come across one in the daytime and the place looks disjointed, vacant as the shine from broken glass in the parking lot. It says a lot about Temperance Hill that the lone club seen from the road is off in a corner by the highway at the far edge of the community. It looks disused. The name on the wall is Ludicrous Lounge.

———

INTERSTATE 73 has been sold in Dillon and Marion Counties as a hurricane evacuation route and a boon to development, which is not to be confused with a boondoggle. This is the road they say will bring the prosperity of the coast to the straggling sandhill and Pee Dee communities. In Latta, that's so funny they can hardly stand it.

"Built for one thing, to funnel people in and out of that beach," says Joe's friend Charles Lane. "I told them it'd be a whole lot cheaper just to put speakers up and down the beach saying, 'Hey, it's a hurricane coming. Everybody leave.'"

Plans call for one exit ramp in Latta. One. Meanwhile, whole communities will be shoved aside. Joe's church, Spring Grove, needs more room. There are plans to build a new sanctuary on the little fork-in-the-road wedge of land owned by the congregation, but the plans are on hold until the leaders can be sure just where the interstate will go.

A number of families will be displaced, including friends of the Lanes that Charles sold land to a few years back on the edge of his holdings. They've built a big country house on a wide lot with a garden farm. The first set of plans Lane was shown called for the stakes to come right through his family's house. He brought his own set of maps to the meeting, ones that showed a line of church and family cemeteries along the route. They moved the road.

"It's going to tear this community up. It's going to come right through, right over on the other side of those woods," Charles Lane says. "You've got the Marion County politicians saying, 'Oh, think of the jobs it's going to bring.' It ain't going to bring diddly squat to Marion County. I got right in the center of his face. I said, 'You know in order to bring jobs to someplace you've got to have a reliable workforce. Half the Marion County workforce is not working. They can't spell 'cat.' They can't count the number of fingers they have on their hands. You get some of these people into some training somewhere, somehow, and make them quit selling drugs up and down the street, you might get somebody to come in here accidental. But it ain't going to be because of I-73. You get fifty miles from that salt-water line and people ain't gonna stop for Marion County.'"

The politician didn't hear the half of it. The road building will cost Marion taxpayers upwards of $50 million per year, Lane continues. He jokes about being able to buy a stretch of the road for that money, to put up a toll booth to get it back. Because that's the only way he sees that Marion County ever will. The project will put people to work building the road, but those aren't permanent jobs. Latta will get a few gas stations, maybe a Hardee's fast-food hamburger place, he said. Those aren't jobs that will help Latta. Lane shakes his head just to think about it. If you'd have told him twenty years ago they would build an interstate through Latta he would have laughed at you. Nothing was coming through Latta anymore. Country folks don't hop on the highway to go to the beach; they know the more peaceful, prettier two-lanes that will get them there.

The idea is to raise the tax on gasoline in Marlboro, Dillon, Horry, and Marion Counties to pay for the road, add another 2 or 4 percent per gallon. When planners came to him to see whether he'd sell his land, he snorted at them: Use my tax money to pay me for my land? The people just don't want the road, he said. But the people don't have much voice.

"Just the ones with the money," he said. "I won't give you no government money to buy an acre of my land, not for no interstate, not if I don't need or like you. I'll sell you a place to build a little house. I don't want your land for no highway. We've got enough roads around here. I can get anywhere in the world from that road right out in front of my house. Might take a little longer to get there. But I can go anywhere in the world starting right there out my driveway."

———

A LOT OF THE PEOPLE who graduated from high school with Joe went north to work. In the still not-so-desegregated 1970s of the Pee Dee, that's where the opportunity was. His generation made up what historians now like to call one of the last waves of the Great Migration. It's also called the Great Black Migration, the mega-movement of people south to north in the early and mid-twentieth century. It may have been, as billed, the biggest face changer and game changer in the distribution of the population of the nation until that time.

The significance wasn't widely regarded for years: The working-class rubes just weren't seen as important enough to make much impact on a culture, never mind, say, music, sports, literature, physics. But there's more to the lack of regard than that. Like a lot of country-ways phenomena, the migration just wasn't so significant to the families who took part in it. It got lost in the whole "Era" approach of looking at American history because it wasn't ever a formal movement. Nobody launched it, nobody claimed it. People just went looking for jobs, one by one, a lot of people. In family after family, somebody who was displaced, disenfranchised, or just disgusted got up and left for greener pastures. If greener meant more money, that meant north. The more folks who went and at least seemed to prosper, the more family members went after them.

It's tough in today's cheap-jet-flight world to imagine the romance of a trip to New York, Detroit, or Philadelphia for a poor Carolinas farm kid, even as recently as the 1970s. Joe says about one acquaintance of his, "When he'd come home we always had to listen to him. Fourth of July, Christmas. He's come home with a real new Cadillac, drive the family around."

The late North Carolina journalist Dwayne Walls, in *The Chickenbone Special,* wrote about what drove Donnie Gibson as a young man from his South Carolina farm home near Salters, little more than fifty miles from Latta: "He wanted to see Central Park almost as much as he wanted to see Hawaii. There would be a chance to see the Mets and all the skyscrapers."

Gibson couldn't get any more than "we'll see" looking for mill work in rural Salters, and those jobs weren't paying $2 per hour. Jobs in New York paid $2 to $3 per hour. He had brothers and sisters in the Big City who told him to come. For Gibson, like a lot of the other nomads, the move away from kith, kin. and countryside wasn't thought of as a move away from family or as anything permanent. One of his sisters already had come back; the city wasn't for her.

Walls writes: "But I don't have to like it, Donnie reasoned. I don't have to stay. I can visit, and if I find a job I'll take it. If I don't like it, I'll come back home."

By the 1970s, so many families in the Pee Dee had relatives "up north" that it wasn't anything at all for Queen Gordon to visit from Pennsylvania or for Joe to be introduced to Celestine from New York.

The "migration" wasn't a black phenomenon; poor whites left too. And the truth of it is that blacks had been leaving the South for as long as they could, tens of thousands in the middle of the Civil War alone. It's just that in the twentieth century the numbers spiked. And that changed the face of things in northern cities. White people, in other words, noticed.

The Great Black Migration usually gets pinned on World War I for cutting off the urban import of cheap foreign laborers, who had to be replaced, especially once the United States started gearing up for the fighting: There was money to be made. Recruiters went south and actively pitched for the workers, as the historian Gerald Early has noted. Hundreds of thousands made the move. But, as Early points out, the truth is a lot subtler than that. In the years before the war, the cotton economy tanked, fields were flooded out in heavy rains, and crop after crop ended up in the bellies of boll weevils. World War I put the spur to a migration already under way. It wasn't so much a migration as a diaspora or maybe just a cliché: Country folk packed up the suitcase and headed out for the Big City. Before the post–World War II industrial boom and the coming-into-its-own of the middle class, the cities with jobs waiting were in the already industrialized north. The choice was to try your luck there or try to elbow your way into and then keep a job cleaning floors among loud, lint-spewing machines in a nearby mill, putting up with backbiting nepotism and kith-and-kin ownership management that laid off the lintheads when work slowed at all to keep from disturbing the family cash cow.

The escape-from-racism argument as a cause doesn't really fly either. Racism can be as prickly in the North as in the South—to this day—and sometimes uglier, with people packed together and jobs at stake. The only real difference was that racism in the North wasn't so often in your face. The discrimination was just as real.

The people who moved came home when they could, like Queen Gordon. So, for the extended families, the "movement" was just a farther version of what was happening in the farmland anyhow—longer and longer commutes to find work, often with makeshift housing during the week and trips home on the weekend. If you wanted to get off the farm and out of the mill, your choices had become jobs like over-the-road trucking or construction-crew labor that followed the contracts. In the late twentieth century, maids and other low-wage staff commuted to the resort hotels of Hilton Head Island by bus from as far as Barnwell County, one hundred miles one way. Any paycheck was that valuable.

By Joe's generation, people all across the region were visiting and sometimes moving among family members up north. The civil-rights-era traumas and social freedoms of the '60s spurred a smaller wave of migration, even as blacks and whites were beginning to come back home and Southern cities were coming into their own. Within the next few decades, you were as likely to hear somebody had left for Atlanta as New York or Chicago.

———

JOE HAD A GREAT-UNCLE who worked in a steel mill in Pittsburgh. When Joe graduated, his uncle told him, come on up. We can get you a job here. Joe thought hard about it. Asked thirty years later why he didn't, he still thinks it over a moment. He was with the Moodys, he says. He stayed.

"I'm glad I didn't [go]. I'm glad I stuck it out. I can look back now, and some of them are moving back now. I accumulated a little something. What I would have accumulated going north, I don't know."

———

JOE CAN STAND on his back porch and point to where the interstate will go through Temperance Hill.

"We've got a lot of people that are homestead-type people. They don't know that much. It's coming. It's coming. Temperance Hill is a very close-knit community, it's a good place to live, it sure is. But it's coming and there ain't nothing you can do about it. It's on the way. Matter of fact they were doing some surveying work last week. It's going to run right behind this house back here, matter of fact."

The road won't kick Joe out, he tells you, not until he can stand on his back porch and see it. The most troubling part is, that's not so far-fetched a possibility. But Joe won't go anywhere, his friend Charles Lane says. "He's got too much dirt under his fingernails, just like me. You couldn't run us off from this. It's home. The only thing we've ever known. Just got too much sand in our shoes to leave."

———

THE OLD DAYS of farming are about gone. Today, manufacturing plants and subdivisions stand where corn and cotton used to rise. Weirdly enough, the number of farms in South Carolina is growing. But the new farms are a motley mix of sprawling, high-tech agribusiness operations and small, specialty-crop niche farms.

"The farm business now is very, very, very technical," banker Walt Brown says. "It's so scientific now that a lot of folks have to really, really work."

U.S. Rep. Jim Clyburn and others are pushing biofuel farms of crops like switchgrass, but the farmers are sitting on their hands to wait and see. Until they can bring it down to the warehouse and get a check, they're not going to buy in. Their fingers have been stepped on too many times already. Joe's thousand acres of leased land don't get you anywhere anymore but behind in payments.

"You put money in and you lose your right hand," Joe says.

CHARLES LANE drifts into the "born two hundred years too late" plaint that you could hear echo throughout the Carolina pinelands as development bull-dozed through in the late twentieth century and people who loved the ageless land watched it get torn up all to hell by people who thought they knew what it was worth. Charles can see himself rocking away on a plantation porch.

"I could have been a fine Southern gentleman," he says. Which is funny, because he is. But the really funny thing to him is how he and Joe stuck with farming as everyone else backed out. He'd just as soon go down to the farmers market to buy produce, he says. Save a lot of sweat.

"What happened to farming? That's a good question." Lane gets a long look on his face. There's not one simple answer. When he and Joe came up, they spent summers out in the rain working cotton. Nowadays if there's no thunder-storm there's no rain. Nobody here wants to talk about climate warming; the region has always been fickle with rain, flood years followed by drought years. In upper Dorchester County farther south, an historical treasure is a diary kept by David Gavin, a plantation owner in the years before, during, and after the Civil War. One of the things in the entries that strikes you is how, from season to season, if Gavin's not griping about how wet it is, he's griping about how dry it is.

But there's more.

"In some cases the farmers overextended themselves," Lane says. "They would get all the money they wanted and were paying a high price of interest on it. That helped take them down. Buy land that there ain't no way you could farm the price of it out of it. Prices fell off on the cotton. I mean, it was just a whole gang of things and everything's working against them. Fuel going up. I'd say farming was in its prime around here, what, up until the '70s, early '70s, and then it ran off the cliff."

It used to be you could buy a farm for $700 or $800 an acre and work off the debt without taking your whole life to do it. Nowadays, the people working tobacco are sitting on the acres, taking that buy-out money and buying more tobacco land.

"There are people in Marion County now spending $3,000 dollars an acre for it," Lane says. "They never work it out of it; they're just tying up some of that money the government's giving them to help them on their taxes. The poor fellow who's trying to farm, he's just catching it. The farmer is at the mercy of the whole world, and God. He's got to sell his product for what the man down the road says he'll get. He can't say, hey, I want $2 a pound for my tobacco. He can't do that. I've got to have $1 a pound for my cotton. He can't do that. The man says I can give you fifty-five cents for that cotton, that's all he's gonna get. The market, the Chicago Board of Trade or whatever, that dictates it. Don't matter if he paid seventy-five cents for it."

So, under one crippling pricing structure after another, with profiteering eating into it, the whole works gradually fell in like a termite-ridden barn. Not that the import-stocked suburbs paid any mind—until 2008. And when that Great Recession hit the Pee Dee family farms it was the roof coming down.

"It was like the Depression," Jimmy Moody said. Having plowed through the farm loan sinkhole and winched himself back from bankruptcy, Joe found the lug nuts popping off.

"It froze everything down. You couldn't get money. Your credit had to be perfect. It froze everything down when you're trying to do something," Joe said. Farming was done. "My hands have been shrunk up I've worked so hard."

——————

JOE COUNTS the days until he closes in on that pension check, and he talks about finally quitting the mill when Angelica gets out of school. He wants to help Little Joe in the funeral-home business. But he still wistfully eyes the fields. If he could do it over, he'd change one thing.

"I would have stayed with my farming more. I would have stayed right on top of it. I spread myself a little thin at times, that's what I've done."

——————

BUT JOE CAME THROUGH all right. Those twenty-five prime farm acres he has on Dudley Road, the old Betsy Turner place that was his first intact farm, rather than just land. After he bought it in that wild, refinance-the-bankruptcy, twenty-four-hour-long workday scramble in 1988, he farmed under an agreement that Mrs. Turner could live there until she died. She was a gristly white farm woman in her eighties who chewed tobacco. When he rode up to put the tractor in the field, she would come out on the back stoop to watch with a plug in her mouth, spitting on the yard, maybe a little bemused at what life had wrought.

"Hey, boy," she'd call out. And Joe would wave. As mentioned before, the Turner place gave him his own curing barn and a second storage barn. It says something about Joe that when he married, he traded in the old woody station wagon for a '63 Ford Fairlane, one of the old pounding-engine muscle cars, with a retractable roof. Naturally he still has it, thirty-seven years later. It sits under a shed at the farm.

The Turner homestead is one of those simple white clapboard one-story farm homes, much like the old Moody place itself. It's surrounded by the ubiquitous pecan trees with a sprawling mimosa out front. The step up to the door is brick. The only fancy touch to be seen from the road is the store-bought wrought iron pillars holding up the porch roof, a decorative winding pattern of leafs.

But the farmhouse says a lot about country heritage and about the extraordinary in the ordinary. From the outside it's plain. Step inside and it takes your breath away. The floors are hardwood. The cabinetry is crafted hardwood. Joe runs his hand over it as he admires it. He's fixing it up as a homestead for Little Joe.

JOE STILL FARMS the forty-six acres up on Ebenezer Road that were once owned by his great-great-grandfather, Scipio Williams. He likes to tell an odd story about it. Joe's not a dog guy; in fact, there are no cats or dogs in the Williams household. But one morning just about daybreak, he had gotten up to take Little Joe to school. Seven black puppies came nosing up the drive. One of them came straight to the door and scratched.

"Right where I'm living at now. And I thought, doggone it, somebody might have thrown out some doggone dogs up here again," he said. Copeland Moody Road is just far enough out of town and its wooded bottoms past Joe's house just thick and isolated enough that the road has become one of those toss-the-litter-off-the-bridge abandonment spots. People can easily delude themselves that, after all, it's the country: Somebody will take them in.

While Joe was mulling what to do about it this time, the other six dogs went to the backyard by the big pecan tree and lay down—"just like you took all six of the puppies and set them up, just like I lay my sleeve, in a line. All six of them." Then another pup came to the door. Joe told Little Joe to fetch his BB gun, the standard, nonlethal discouragement for varmints in the countryside.

"Let me sting these dogs and they'll run," Joe said. "I'm sick of people dropping dogs out here." Little Joe told him, "The gun won't shoot, Daddy." Joe lost his temper and demanded that Little Joe give him the gun. But Little Joe was right; the gun wouldn't shoot. "And I felt strange about that thing. I felt strange. And I prayed about that thing. And I went to work that night and it come to me." Those dogs were a sign that his great-great-granddaddy had come back to thank him for getting some of the family land back.

That's odd, all right. As a "sign," it leaves you asking, why dogs? Why seven? But a BB gun that shot the time before and would shoot the next time didn't shoot. Joe is convinced. He tells the story again and says again about the land, "I hope that Joe Junior or Angelica will want to hold it just as long as they will. That's where they originated from."

———

JOE'S JUST AN OLD HOMESTEAD PERSON, he says. He's always believed in leaving farmland as farmland and leaving woods as woodland. Part of that is traditional farmland management, back in the days when you needed the wood for winter fires just about as much as you needed the crops for food. But there's more to it. Joe has that almost spiritual tie to the land you find in anyone who loves the outdoors.

"If I cut wood I set it out again. That's just my belief," Joe says. "One thing, I don't care if hell freezes over, I'm going to keep my tractor and my digger. Little Joe, he buries me, he can take it and chuck it in the river. He can chuck it in the river."

———

CHARLES LANE says Joe could have been a multimillionaire if he had been able to buy the Cotton Grove land, if a few other turns in his life had gone another way. His life with Copeland Moody opened up associations with people he wouldn't have met otherwise.

"He knows everybody in the world, and he's run up on some unlikely contacts in his life," Charles says. "He's been good to people, and they've looked out for him and helped out him too."

———

THE MARCH MORNING is cutting cold. Behind the old Moody home irises have come up, wriggling in the wind, around the old trailer where Joe used to live. Irene Moody planted them, her way of gussying up the place for him. Down the driveway along the property line the hedges he planted with her have almost begun to flower.

Joe keeps a can of starter fluid in the cab of the old Farm Op 140, one of three aging tractors sitting in a back lot behind a screen of trees on the land around the old Moody home. Little Joe grabs the can from the cab as he hops up in the seat, tosses it down, and Joe gives the old engine a long spray. Joe rests his arm up on the big tire as he talks.

"OK, Junior," he calls up. The engine grinds, grinds, and catches in a plume of oily smoke. The motor settles into rhythm; the smoke whitens. Joe stands and watches. His eyes seem to hover over the machine. He's wearing a well-worn International Harvester ball cap, work pants, boots, and a thick flannel shirt. Both he and Little Joe wear hoodie sweaters.

It's planting time. They're off to disc nine acres on Scipio Williams's old land for soybeans and corn. The acres sit back in a bowl of hardwoods and pine where scattered redbuds are in bloom. The surroundings have the feel of a huge natural amphitheater.

Joe talks about replacing the ratty seat on the old tractor, the work he needs to do on the front end. When he stops by Dillon Tractor and Implement Co., where he has done business all these years, his eyes rove the line of huge new tractors.

"I want to buy a new one. I want to own [a new] one before I die," he tells Doug Lynn, of the family that owns the place. But Joe just buys parts he needs to keep his old tractors running. A lot of the newer equipment isn't built to last like it used to be. Joe's old equipment, Lynn will tell you, "is almost bulletproof."

After the tractor rumbles its way down to the field, Little Joe turns the first rows. Joe watches, pacing a little, gazing up at the trees then turning back to follow the tractor, looking for all the world like a coach on the sidelines.

"If I had a thousand acres this place would mean more to me," Joe says. "I can see Grandpa back here hauling mules."

Joe's debt on his land is in the short rows now. He talks about getting the funeral home going, getting a bigger daycare for Celeste, then kicking back and enjoying some grand young'uns.

"I took my beatings," Joe says and nods the cap toward his son "He's the next generation behind me. It's left up to him." But he knows farming for Little Joe won't be the passion it was for him. "I'm kind of glad it isn't in his blood."

Joe signals in his son. It's his turn now. He doesn't climb into the tractor so much as sling himself in. He turns to look behind him at the positioning of the discs. He gives it a long look. Then he turns back, clicks the tractor into gear, and doesn't look back again. At the finish of a row the tractor seems to spin in place to line up the next row. He doesn't look back.

ACROSS OLD EBENEZER ROAD, there's an aroma like sweet grass in the air. Green shivers shimmy in the breeze across fourteen acres around the site of the old Scipio Williams homeplace. The blades of new wheat are sticky to the touch. Joe knows about where the tongue-and-groove carpentered home stood, but not exactly. When he works the field he finds bits of old brick and debris and wonders if they came from Scipio's hand.

"This is it," as Little Joe says, "this is where the Williamses got started."

The old Scipio Williams house would have been a sight to see. For a man raised among planter manors, you can imagine, a man who earned freedom with his hands, the house was his stake in new ground, his way of counting coup, of saying I am here.

Joe has that reverential feel for this field that people get when they love their land. You can see it in the way he walks the rows. It reminds you of pews. Sometimes, in the twilight after sunset, as he begins to call it a day, he can feel Granddad Scipio walking there with him.

"I tell him, I'm trying to get your land back for you. I ain't got all of it. But I've got some of it."

Sources

Abraham Lincoln Papers. Library of Congress, www.loc.gov. April 16, 2014.

Bethea, Christopher Lynn. "A History of Latta, Home of Champions." Self-published, 1974.

The Black Farmers and Agriculturalists Association website. www.bfaa-us.org. April 16, 2014.

"Boating Guide to the Little Pee Dee." South Carolina Department of Natural Resources, http://www.dnr.sc.gov/water/river/pdf/LittlePeeDeeTrailGuide.pdf. April 16, 2014.

Cape Fear Arch Conservation Collaboration. www.capefeararch.org. April 16, 2014.

Congressional Research Service. www.loc.gov/crsinfo. April 16, 2014.

Cooney, John. "Preserving a Nation." *Obitmag.com.* April 17, 2014.

Dorsi, Joseph. "Architecture of American Homes, 17th and 18th Century." Bryant University, Smithfield, R.I. http://web.bryant.edu/~ehu/h364proj/sprg_98/dorsi/index.htm. April 16, 2014

Drake Journal of Agricultural Law. Drake University, Des Moines, Iowa. Reprinted on the Farmers Legal Action Group website, www.flaginc.org. April 16, 2014.

Edgar, Walter. *South Carolina a History.* Columbia: University of South Carolina Press, 1998.

"The Embalming Process and Welcome to Embalming, 101." You Tube, http://www.youtube.com. April 16, 2014.

Environmental Working Group 2011 Farm Subsidy Database. www.farm.ewg.org. April 16, 2014.

Foner, Eric. *The Fiery Trial: Abraham Lincoln and American Slavery.* New York. W. W. Norton, 2010.

Georgia Historical Society. www. http://georgiahistory.com. April 16, 2014.

Johnson, Michael P., and James L. Roark. *Black Masters: A Free Family of Color in the Old South.* New York: W. W. Norton, 1984.

Journal of Southern History. www.jsh.rice.edu. April 16, 2014.

Keckley, Elizabeth. *Behind the Scenes, or Thirty Years as a Slave and Four Years in the White House.* New York: Oxford University Press, 1988.

The Lincoln Institute. www.lincolnedu.com. April 16, 2014.

National Black Farmers Association. www.blackfarmers.org. April 16, 2014.

National Park Service. www.nps.gov. April 16, 2014.

National Register of Historic Places. http://www.cr.nps.gov/nr. April 16, 2014.

New Georgia Encyclopedia. Georgia Humanities Council, http://www.georgiaencyclopedia.org. April 16, 2014.

Pike, James S. *The Prostrate State: South Carolina under Negro Government.* 1873. Public domain.

[Charleston] Post and Courier. www.postandcourier.com. April 17, 2014.

Prince, Eldred E. Jr., and Robert R. Simpson. *Long Green: The Rise and Fall of Tobacco in South Carolina*. Athens: University of Georgia Press, 2000.

South Carolina State Climatology Office. http://www.dnr.sc.gov/climate/sco. April 16, 2014.

South Carolina Wildlife magazine. www.scwildlife.com., April 16, 2014.

Stokes, Durwood T. *The History of Dillon County*. Columbia: University of South Carolina Press, 1978.

Sullivan Press. www.SullivanPress.com. April 16, 2014.

U.S. Geological Survey. www.usgs.gov. April 16, 2014.

University of Georgia website, www.uga.edu. April 16, 2014.

Walls, Dwayne. *The Chickenbone Special*. San Diego: Harcourt Brace Jovanovich, 1973.

Index

Abraham Lincoln Research Site (http://rogerjnorton.com/Lincoln2.html), 48

Allotments. *See* Farm subsidies and allotments

Andrews Chapel United Methodist Church (Latta, SC), 55

Anglo-African Weekly, 48, 55

Architecture of American Homes (Dorsi), 10

Army Corps of Engineers (U.S.), 105

Asbury, Francis (preacher), 7

ASCR. *See* Assistant Secretary for Civil Rights

Ashley River (SC), 4, 96

Assistant Secretary for Civil Rights (ASCR), 88, 89

Autopsies, 126, 129. *See also* Funerals

Avery Research Center (College of Charleston), 56

Bartell, Flossie (Sam Bartell's wife), 128–30

Bartell's Funeral Home, 128, 129

Bartell, Sam (funeral home owner), 128–29

Bays, 4, 71, 72, 74, 106–07, 108

Beach, the. *See* Myrtle Beach

Becote, Ruby (Celestine Williams' first cousin), 72, 73

Berlin, Irv (historian), 56

Bethea, Bob R. (storekeeper, postmaster), 40

Bethea, Christopher Lynn (author), 135

Bethea cotton press, 7f, 8, 40, 121

Bethea, John (farmer; "Buck Swamp"), 40

Bethea, John, III (builder of cotton press), 8, 121

Bethea plantation, 40

Big Pee Dee. *See* Great Pee Dee River

Black Farmers and Agriculturalists Association, 89

Black farm-loan scandal. *See* Farm-loan scandal

Black Masters: A Free Family of Color in the Old South (Johnson and Roark), 54

Blacks: as Civil War spies, 52; lynching of, 93; Native Americans and, 119–20; payback of loans by, 102; as politicians, 92; population of, 92; white visitors of, 17–18. *See also* Great Black Migration; Racial bias and racism; Segregation and integration; Whites

Boise Cascade Cooperation, 74

Boise Cascade timberlands, 1, 74, 108

Booth, John W., 26

Boyd, John (farmer), 89, 90

Brown vs. Board of Education (1954), 37

Brown, Walt (banker), 78, 97, 141

Brush arbors. *See* Churches

Bryant, J. G. (farmer; Joe's mentor), 5, 43, 75, 84

Buck Swamp (SC), 121

Campbell, Emory (researcher, historian), 55

Camp meetings. *See* Revivals

Cape Fear Arch (NC-SC), 4, 135

Cape Romain (SC), 4

Carmichael, B. F. (school superintendent, coach), 63–64

Carolina Bays, 71, 74

Carolinas, 96. *See also* North Carolina; South Carolina

Carter, Jimmy, 75

Catfish Baptist Church (Latta, SC), 6

Charleston (SC), 4, 40, 105

Charleston News and Courier, The, 93

Charlotte (NC), 105

Cheraw (SC), 86–87

Chickenbone Special, The (Walls), 139

Chiriqui colony (Brazil), 51

Churches, 6–8. *See also* Revivals (camp meetings)

Churches-specific: Andrews Chapel United
Methodist Church (Latta, SC), 55; Catfish
Baptist Church (Latta, SC), 6; Ebenezer
Southern Methodist Church (Marion, SC),
16; Spring Grove Baptist Church (outside
Latta, SC), 6, 34, 137
Cigarettes and smoking, 79–80. *See also*
Tobacco
Civil rights era (1960s), 140
Civil War (U.S.; 1861–1865), 5, 51–52, 54–55, 92,
131, 139. *See also* Lincoln, Abraham
Clardy, Sam (teacher, minister), 65
Cleveland, Grover, 40
Climate, 96–97, 107–08, 111, 142
Clyburn, James (D-SC; "Jim"), 142
Collington, Isaiah (Joe's school principal), 39
Colonization. *See* Resettlement and coloniza-
tion
Contraband camps (Washington, DC), 51
Cooney, John (writer), 131–32
Copeland Moody house, 13, 75–76
Copeland Moody Road, 14, 69, 144
Corn, 3, 57–58, 72, 78, 98, 141, 146
Cotton brokers, 100, 101
Cotton Grove plantation, 1, 74, 84, 145
Cotton farming and picking, 26–28, 54–57, 62,
95, 98, 140, 142
Cotton gins, 100
"Croatans," 38–39
Crop lien law, 94–95
Crop rotation, 98
Crump, Leon (farmer, Vietnam veteran),
86–89, 91, 92

Daniel, Pete (historian), 83–84
Department of Agriculture (USDA; U.S.), 81,
83–86, 88–90, 97, 101–02
Department of Justice (DOJ; U.S.), 89–90
Dillon (SC), 57
Dillon County (SC), 37, 62, 64, 84, 105, 121, 137
Dillon Tractor and Implement Co., 146
DOJ. *See* Department of Justice
Dorchester County (SC), 7
Dorsi, Joseph (author), 10
Douglass, Frederick (black abolitionist and
preacher), 52
Drake Journal of Agricultural Law, 91

Early, Gerald (historian), 140
Earthquake of 1886, 4, 25, 56

Ebenezer Southern Methodist Church
(Marion, SC), 16, 46
Edgar, Walter (historian), 53, 55, 92, 93, 94, 95
Ellison, William (freedman), 54
Ellsworth, Elmer (lawyer), 131
El Niño/La Niña, 96, 97
Emancipation Proclamation (January 1, 1863),
51
Embalming, 129–32. *See also* Funerals
Epps, Clement "Olin" (school principal),
22–23, 63–64

Family members-Moody: Moody, Amanda
(Jimmy's daughter), 43; Moody, Copeland
(Irene's husband, Jimmy's father), 13–19,
31–34, 39, 43–46, 63, 64, 67, 69, 74, 77, 121,
122, 126, 145; Moody, Irene (Copeland's
wife, Jimmy's mother), 44, 46, 69–70, 75,
76, 108, 122, 145; Moody, Jimmy (Copeland's
son), 14–16, 19–20, 26, 31–36, 39, 43–45,
63–64, 121, 143; Moody, Randy (Copeland's
son), 64
Family members-Williams: Aunt Blanche,
27–28, 32; Collington, Isaiah (Joe's cousin),
39; Gordon, Queen (Joe's cousin), 18–19,
24, 25, 49, 53–54, 109; Joe's father, 11–12;
Lane, Charles (Joe's cousin), 22; Lane,
Minnie (Joe's great-great-grandmother),
6, 25–26; Matlock, Shirley Cribb (Joe's
cousin), 21; McKay, Earlene Williams (Joe's
older sister), 26, 27–28, 38, 44; Williams,
Albert (Joe's great-grandfather), 10, 11, 29;
Williams, Angelica (Joe's daughter), 68, 76,
112–13, 114–15; Williams, Catherine Tuluder
(Scipio's sixth child; Aunt Lou), 11, 23–25,
47, 48, 53, 55, 58, 59; Williams, Celestine
(Joe's wife; "Celeste"), 72–73, 76, 112;
Williams, Edward (Scipio's eldest child),
59–60; Williams, Fanny (Scipio's daughter),
59; Williams, Frank (Scipio's son), 58; Williams, Fred (Joe's grandfather), 9, 10; Williams, John F. Kennedy (Joe's baby brother;
deceased), 128; Williams, Judy (Joe's sister
and twin), 11–12, 26–28; Williams, Laura
Crawford (Scipio's wife; Joe's great-great-
grandmother), 24, 53, 57, 109, 125; Williams,
Little Joe (Joe's son), 35, 73, 76, 77, 113–14,
115, 130, 143, 144–46; Williams, Melvin
(Joe's brother), 62. *See also* Williams, Geraldine; Williams, Joe; Williams, Scipio

Farming and farm work, 27, 80–81, 93–94, 98, 112, 141–43. *See also* Cotton farming and picking; Sharecropping and sharecroppers; Tobacco; Williams, Joe; *other individual crops*

Farm-loan scandal, 8, 85–95. *See also* Loans and lenders

Farm Service Agency, 91. *See also* Farm-loan scandal

Farm subsidies and allotments, 79, 80–85, 99, 107

Federation of Southern Cooperatives, 86

Felton, Raymond (NBA player), 63

Fertilizer, 80–81, 84, 87, 98, 100–101

Fields, Joseph (farmer), 85

Fiery Trial, The (Foner), 48

Florence Morning Star, 25

Florida, 127

Foner, Eric (historian and author), 48–50

Francis Marion College, 73–74

Francis Marion National Forest, 103

Freedmen: Ellison, William, 54; governments by, 55–56; guardianship law and, 54; as laborers, 94; lands of, 5, 53–53; Lincoln, Abraham and, 47–49, 52, 55, 56; militias of, 56; Pinckney family, 54; during Reconstruction, 92; in Washington, DC, 51, 55; wealth of, 55. *See also* Williams, Joe; Williams, Scipio

Freedmen Bureau, 95

Funerals, 125–33

GAO. *See* General Accounting Office

Gavin, David (plantation owner), 142

Geechee culture, 127

General Accounting Office (GAO; U.S.), 88–89

Georgetown (SC), 120, 121

Georgia, 127

Gibson, Donnie, 139

Glickman, Dan (Secretary of Agriculture), 89

Goodwine, Marquetta (Queen Quet; Gullah/Geechee Coalition founder), 127

Gordon, Queen (Joe's cousin), 18–19, 24, 49, 53–54, 109

Graylyn Mansion (Winston-Salem, NC), 80

Great Black Migration, 138–40

Great Migration, 138–41

Great Pee Dee River, 1, 2, 117–18, 119–21

Great Recession (2008), 90, 143

Greene, Harlan, 56

Gullah people and communities, 6, 49, 55–56, 126–27

Hamer, P.B. (judge), 60

Hilton Head Island (SC), 140

Hispanics, 119–20

History of Marion County (Sellers), 23

Holmes, Thomas (doctor, coroner), 131–32

"Home of Champions" (manuscript; Bethea), 135

Houghton Library (Harvard University), 48

Hurricane Hugo (1989), 13–14, 103–05

Hurricane of 1870s, 103

Hurricane of 1893, 56

Hurricane route, 137

Hurricanes (general), 104

International Paper, 121

Interstate-73, 135, 137–38, 141

Interstate-95, 135

Jackson, Andrew, 119

Jackson, Samuel (embalmer), 126

Jim Crow era (1890s), 40

Johnson, Alex (high school assistant principal), 5

Johnson, Michael P. (author), 54

Jones, Frank (former mayor), 124–25

Journal of Southern History, 83–84

Keckley, Elizabeth (Mrs. Lincoln's dressmaker), 52

KKK *See* Ku Klux Klan

Kingdom of Oyotunji (SC), 49

King, Martin Luther, Jr., 18

Kingstree (SC), 94

Kirby, John (school superintendent; Vicki's husband), 41–42, 115

Kirby, Vicki (John Kirby's wife), 41

Kolb archeological site (Mechanicsville, SC), 120

Ku Klux Klan (KKK), 40, 93–94

Land: Southern freedmen and, 52–53; cotton and the value of, 54–55; ownership by black farmers, 94; prices of and speculation in, 97; wealth and, 9. *See also* Williams, Joe; Williams, Scipio

Lane, Charles (Joe's cousin and friend), 22, 43, 64, 77, 108, 137, 141–43, 145
Lane, James, 21
Lane, Minnie (Joe's great-great-grandmother), 6, 25–26
La Niña/El Niño, 96, 97
Latta (SC): civil rights protests and, 18; Corridor of Shame and, 37; as a farm and railroad town, 5–6, 40, 79, 99–100, 101, 135; history and naming of, 8, 40, 135; Hurricane Hugo and, 105; Interstate-73 and, 137–38; map of, 2; outdoorsman shop in, 121–22; schools in, 37–38, 39, 41, 42; segregation and integration in, 19, 38, 41–42; sports in, 42, 63; tobacco and, 79. *See also* Churches; Pee Dee region; Temperance Hill
Latta, Robert, 8
Lee, Robert E (Confederate General), 52
Legette, George (Joe's childhood friend), 5, 26, 30, 32, 43, 62, 63, 64, 77, 85
Legislature (SC), 92–93, 94, 95
Lincoln, Abraham ("Abe"): embalming of soldiers and, 131; meeting with Washington ministers, 50–51; opinions and myths of, 5, 47–50, 56; stops at contraband camps and with freedmen, 51; Williams, Scipio and, 3, 25–26. *See also* Civil War; Emancipation Proclamation
Lincoln, Mary Todd (Lincoln's wife), 51, 131
Lincoln, Todd (Lincoln's son; deceased), 132
Little Pee Dee River, 2, 117, 119, 121
Loans and lenders, 57, 81, 85. 87, 90–92, 94–95, 101. *See also* Farm-loan scandal
Long Green: The Rise and Fall of Tobacco in South Carolina (Prince), 54–55, 56, 79, 94
Lost Colony (NC), 38–39
Ludicrous Lounge (Latta, SC), 137
Lumbee tribe, 39
Lynching. *See* Blacks
Lynn, Doug (tractor company owner), 146

Marion County (SC), 21, 40, 53, 55, 64, 74, 84, 92–94, 105, 121, 137–38, 143
Marion, Hester Hunter (slave), 40
Marlboro County (SC), 86–87, 119
Matlock, Shirley Cribb (Joe's cousin), 21
McClellanville (SC), 103
McKay, Earlene Williams (Joe's older sister), 26, 27–28, 44
McSwain, Curt (farmer), 111–12

Mechanicsville (SC), 120
Merchant, Virginia (Copeland Moody's sister; Aunt Ginnie), 1, 45–46, 63, 69, 76
Militias, 56, 94
Monroe, Franklin or Francis Marion (Clement Epps' grandfather), 22, 23
Moody Agri Co., 17, 43, 100–101
Moody, Amanda (Jimmy's daughter), 43
Moody, Copeland (Irene's husband, Jimmy's father), 13–19, 31–34, 39, 43–46, 63, 64, 67, 69, 74, 77, 121, 122, 126, 145. *See also* Copeland Moody house; Copeland Moody Road
Moody, Irene (Copeland's wife, Jimmy's mother), 44, 46, 69–70, 75, 76, 108, 122, 145
Moody, Jimmy (Copeland's son), 14–16, 19–20, 26, 31–36, 39, 43–45, 63–64, 121, 143
Moody, Randy (Copeland's son), 64
Morning Star, 25
Mullins (SC), 41, 42, 57, 79
Myrtle Beach (SC), 135–37

National Black Farmers Association, 89, 90
National Register of Historic Places, 5
Native Americans, 39, 119–20. *See also* "Croatans"
NC. *See* North Carolina
New Georgia Encyclopedia, 127
North (U.S.). *See* Great Migration
North Carolina (NC), 38, 75, 118–19, 120, 135
Norton, Roger, 48

Obama, Barack, 37, 47
Obit Magazine, 131
Okra Point cemetery (Latta, SC), 124, 125
Orangeburg Massacre (SC; 1968), 18
Outer Banks (NC), 38

PA. *See* Pennsylvania
Peas, 24, 32, 72, 73, 114
Pee Dee region: before the Civil War, 54–55; Cape Fear Arch and, 4; cotton in, 100; drought in, 111, 120; environs of, 4; farming in, 71; Hurricane Hugo and, 105; light and heavy land in, 4–5, 71, 84; segregation in, 18–19, 41; tobacco in, 57, 83, 84; traditions of, 6; wage jobs in, 111. *See also* Dillon; Great Pee Dee River; Latta; Little Pee Dee River; Marion County

Pee Dee River. *See* Great Pee Dee River; Little Pee Dee River
Peg-and-stile houses, 10, 22, 25, 108–10, 133
Penn Center (Saint Helena Island, SC), 55
Penn School (Saint Helena Island, SC), 55
Pennsylvania (PA), 18–19
Pigford, Tim (farmer), 89
Pigford v. Glickman (1999), 89
Pike, James S. (author), 92–93
Pinckney Estates, 54, 103
Pinckney, Lucian (descendant of a freedman), 104
Pittsburgh (PA), 141
Post and Courier, The, 85
Powers, T.C. (storekeeper), 8–9
Praise houses. *See* Churches
Prince, Eldred E. (author), 54;-55, 56, 79, 80–81, 83, 94
Prostrate State, The (Pike), 92–93

Queen Quet. *See* Goodwine, Marquetta

Racial bias and racism, 41, 75, 85–86, 90, 119–20, 140. *See also* Blacks; Native Americans; Segregation and integration; Whites
Reconstruction period, 92
Red Hill Cemetery (Sellers, SC), 124–25
Red Raiders (Latta; sports team), 42
Resettlement and colonization, 49–51, 52. *See also* Segregation and integration; Slaves and slavery
Revivals (camp meetings), 6, 7–8. *See also* Churches
Rice and rice growing, 127
Roadhouses, 137
Roark, James L., 54
Rural Advancement (Pittsboro, NC), 87

SAAs. *See* Shared Appreciation Agreements
Saint Helena Island, 49, 55, 127
Savannah (GA), 57
SC. *See* South Carolina
Scandals. *See* Farm-loan scandal
Schneider, Susan A. (lawyer), 91. *See also* Farm-loan scandal
Schools, 37–38, 41–42
Scipio (slave and historical names), 21. *See also* Williams, Scipio
Scipio Williams Memorial Chapel, 132–33
Segregation and integration: in Latta, 19, 38,

41–43; in the Pee Dee region, 18–19, 41–42, 138. *See also* Blacks; Racial bias and racism; Slaves and slavery; Whites
Sellers (SC), 124, 125
Sellers, W.W. (historian, writer), 23
Selma protest march (Alabama; 1965), 18
Sharecroppping and sharecroppers, 93, 94
Shared Appreciation Agreements (SAAs), 91. *See also* Farm-loan scandal
Shouts. *See* Churches
Slaves and slavery, 21, 40, 52, 53, 127, 131. *See also* Blacks; Freedmen; Racial bias and racism; Resettlement and colonization; Segregation and integration; Whites
Smoking. *See* Cigarettes and smoking; Tobacco
South (U.S.). *See* Great Migration; *individual cities, counties, and states*
South Carolina (SC), 18, 24, 37, 49, 52–55, 92–93, 105, 118–20, 127, 136, 141. *See also individual cities, towns, and counties*
South Carolina: A History (Edgar), 53
South Carolina Indian Affairs Commission, 120
South Carolina Tobacco Museum, 79
Soybeans, 3, 72, 78, 98, 112, 146
Spring Grove Baptist Church (outside Latta, SC), 6, 34, 137
Stokes, Durwood (historian), 6
Stoudenmire, Lou (teacher; Seba Stoudenmire's wife), 66–67
Stoudenmire, Seba (teacher, principal; Lou's husband), 66, 67
Subsidies. *See* Farm subsidies and allotments
Sugar cane, 24
Summerville (SC), 96
Sweet potatoes, 3, 78, 98, 107
Switchgrass, 142

Temperance Hill (SC), 8–9, 135, 137, 141. *See also* Latta
Thomas, Edwin (Reverend), 51
Thompson, Ambrose, 51
Tobacco, 57, 75, 79–84, 98, 107, 127, 142
Truth, Sojourner (black abolitionist), 52
Turner, Betsy (owner of Turner farm), 99, 143–44
Turner farm, 97, 99, 112, 143. *See also* Turner, Betsy; Turner, Phillip
Turner, Gary (Boise Cascade supervisor), 74, 75, 108
Turner, Phillip (friend), 99

Uncle Bunk (old man and friend), 34
Union County (SC), 93
USDA. *See* Department of Agriculture

Venus fly traps, 136
Vesey uprising (Charleston, SC; 1822), 40

Walls, Dwayne (journalist), 139
War between the States. *See* Civil War
Watermelon, 98
Wealth. *See* Land
Weather, 96–97, 107–08, 111, 142
Weems, Robert (geologist), 4
West African customs, 127. *See also* Gullah
    people and communities
Whale wallows. *See* Bays
Wheat, 3, 78, 98
Whites: Great Migration and, 139–40; Native
    Americans and, 119–20; population of, 92;
    rapes of white women, 93; visiting black
    homes, 17–18. *See also* Blacks; Racial bias
    and racism; Segregation and integration
Williams, Angelica (Joe's daughter), 68, 76,
    112–13, 114–16
Williamsburg County (SC), 93
Williams, Catherine Tuluder (Scipio's sixth
    child; Aunt Lou), 11, 23–25, 47, 48, 53, 55, 58,
    59, 109
Williams, Celestine (Joe's wife, "Celeste"),
    72–73, 76, 99, 112, 116
Williams, Edward (Scipio's eldest child),
    59–60
Williams, Fanny (Scipio's daughter), 59
Williams, Frank (Scipio's son), 58
Williams, Frank (Joe's brother), 114
Williams, Fred (Joe's grandfather), 9, 10, 11
Williams Funeral Home, 132–33
Williams, Geraldine (Joe's mother) , 109, 126;
    Aunt Lou and, 24, 25; cotton picking and
    fieldwork by, 11, 26–28, 29, 39; family and
    husband of, 29–30, 32–34; funeral custom
    of, 128; home of Williams, Scipio and, 10–11,
    22; as Joe and Judy's mother, 27, 28, 29–30,
    32, 43; Latta schools and, 38; Lincoln,
    Abraham and, 5, 47; Little Joe and, 114;
    photograph of, 29f
Williams, Jarvis M. (freedman petition
    signer), 49
Williams, Joe: bankruptcy of, 97, 99, 102,
    107, 132, 143; Bartell, Sam and Flossie and,

128–29; childhood of, 8, 13, 15–16, 19–20, 23,
    25, 26–28, 29–30, 32, 43–46; church and, 6;
    family life of, 70, 72–73; football and, 64–65,
    114; fraud charges against, 103; funeral
    home and funerals and, 125–31, 132–33, 143;
    home of Williams, Scipio and, 9–10, 31, 108,
    125–26; homes of, 3, 13, 15, 62, 75–76; house
    of, 76; Hurricane Hugo and, 105; injury of,
    102–03; KKK and, 93–94; lawsuit payout
    and, 90–91; Moody Agri Co. work and,
    100–101; Moody, Copeland and, 16–17, 19,
    34, 43–46, 63, 67, 69–70, 74, 77, 122, 126, 145;
    Moody, Irene and, 69–70, 75–76, 108, 122;
    Moody, Jimmy and, 15–16, 19–20, 34–36,
    43; as a parent, 115–16; Pee Dee Rivers and,
    121–22; personality and potential of, 39,
    41, 63, 65, 67, 68, 74, 77–78, 82, 129, 145–46;
    schools and schooling of, 37–38, 39, 41,
    42–43, 62–63, 64, 65–69, 73–74; "whole-hog
    year" (1989) of, 97–99, 102–06, 107; Wil-
    liams, Scipio and, 3, 123; work and farming
    of, 1, 3–4, 8, 29–31, 65, 71–72, 77–79, 81–82,
    84–85, 97–99, 102, 106–07, 109–12, 142,
    145–47. *See also* Family members; Moody,
    Copeland; Moody, Jimmy
Williams, John F. Kennedy (Joe's baby
    brother; deceased), 128
Williams, Judy (Joe's sister and twin), 11–12,
    26–28
Williams, Laura Crawford (Scipio's wife;
    Joe's great-great-grandmother), 24, 53, 109,
    125
Williams, Little Joe (Joe's son), 35, 73, 76–77,
    113–16, 125–26, 130, 132, 143–46
Williams, Melvin (Joe's brother), 62
Williams, Scipio (Joe's great-great-grand-
    father): childhood of, 22–23, 49; children
    of, 9; farm, house, and land of, 9–10, 22, 25,
    53–54, 57–59, 77, 95, 108, 109–10, 123, 144; as
    a freedman, 53, 55–56; grave of, 125; Letters
    Testamentary of, 57–60, 95, 125; Lincoln,
    Abraham, and, 3, 25–26, 47, 60; photograph
    of, 109; as a tailor and carpenter, 25, 54, 56,
    125–26, 133; Williams, Joe and, 3. *See also*
    Scipio
Woodbury, Millie J. (teacher), 66, 67–68
World War I (1914–1918), 140
World War II (1939–1945), 140

Yazoos, 117